THE ANIMAL VERSE

Escape the Flood with the Second Coming of Great Noah

Great
NOAH AGROTES

CONTENTS

PREFACE

Dear reader,

Have you ever looked around you and felt that something was seriously wrong?

That this world is broken and rotten?

That your fellow humans are disgusting and irrational?

If so, then you are not wrong. This pitiful world, this disgusting civilisation, is doomed. I noticed this a long time ago, and I first warned humankind of this in my previous book "The Temple of Consciousness". However, as I expected, nothing changed. Humans didn't care and certainly didn't change their path of fate.

Now, the time is slipping ever nearer to the end of civilisation and we will experience a flood — just like the Great Flood of ancient times — albeit not a literal flood of water but a flood of people, as you will see later in this book.

In the Great Flood, Noah built a boat and loaded the animals two by two, as the story goes. In today's eminent flood, this Great Noah will lead a select few in a different, more elegant, method of escape.

In my previous book, I explained how you can join the Evolutionary Way to become an evolved being, which showed you the path to escape this fate.

In this book, you will learn more about this disgusting world, and you will gain more tools to help you become an evolved being.

Do you wish to evolve and become one of the Greats or continue as a human animal in this brutal, primal Animal Verse? For the Greats, the unavoidable end of our civilisation doesn't mean a thing. The Greats will continue in the Conscious Verse. The Greats will continue to expand elsewhere, long after the human animal species kills itself off.

Yours sincerely,

Great Noah

WELCOME TO THE ANIMAL VERSE

Welcome to The Animal Verse, dear reader!

Of course, you are already living in The Animal Verse, though you are not aware of this — probably because nobody has ever told you that's where you are. Nobody ever handed you a map filled with squalor and a pin saying "you are here".

In the pages of this book, you will be shown around The Animal Verse for the first time ever, given a guided tour of this horrible place where you are consigned to live.

In this place, you arrived as a baby, and you knew nothing. As you grew up, you became a slave in mind to what you were told, a slave in life to the power of money, and a slave in time to the system and ways of work. What's more, you were totally blind to and ignorant of the conditions and powers that applied against you. You went to school and got a 9-5 job. Maybe you got married and had children or spent your time searching for "the one".

At first, you didn't stop to question anything, but when you started to, the questions seemed to lead nowhere and result in no answers. If you shared your thoughts and concerns with anyone, they said you were eccentric or cynical. Your fellow humans seemed oblivious to your plight.

But now, you are awake and you want answers. You don't care what your fellow humans think. Perhaps you don't even see them as your fellows at all, and don't feel like a human.

The problem is, you are stuck here in this Animal Verse, living amongst the other animals. You are a human animal, living a life little better than an animal, and in some cases far worse than an animal. Humans are directed like cattle to have certain beliefs and are hemmed in like sheep to not fight back.

And so, you are an animal… or an animal's equal.

Like the other animals, the human animal acts from their base instincts, but worse than the other animals, they often act from their emotions. They were gifted with the greatest tools: consciousness and logic, but they choose to ignore or abandon these tools in favour of their flawed, irrational, and overzealous emotions. This is why their behaviour is often flawed and base.

I will spread in front of you some histories of how our stupid, dirty species acts within the Animal Verse — histories that may shock you because there is no animal out there dirtier in body and mind than the human animal. While some people might call pigs dirty, or hippos, or dung beetles, you will see in this book that humans are by far the dirtiest animal. for example, you will learn about the disgusting and little-known Sexual Holocaust that occurred in Southern Cyprus.

On our journey around The Animal Verse, this is your map:

In Part 1, you will get a brief alternate history of humans… from the conception of consciousness to the development of modern societies.

You will see into the future regarding the search for alien life and artificial intelligence.

You will understand more about the human sexual animal and the sham of marriage.

And you will discover secrets about the lesser-known world of lucid dreaming and the Mormon church.

In Part 2, you will find out more about the dark power ruling our world, the hidden forces at play.

You'll understand the human animal concept of time, which explains why the human animal is stuck of a straight-line velocity going nowhere, and why our species is stagnating.

You will get a grand unified theory of Europe including an alternate history of the two previous world wars, the current war in Ukraine, and the battlefields of the third stage of the world war, which we are already though the human animal does not realise this.

Finally, you will see my theory of the Eurozone and the productive identity of people living and working in Europe, which is being increasingly devalued.

These factors will lead to the collapse of human civilisation, starting in Europe and leading to the end of the entire Animal Verse.

So, get ready, dear reader, to discover some of the most astonishing and shocking histories ever. Get ready to become more awake than 99.9% of your fellow humans.

When you become fully awake and on the path of the Greats, you will understand the creative peace and freedom available to you.

Unlike the human animal, the Greats are not ruled by their base emotions. They are not trapped like you and your fellow animals in a physical body, in this awful physical place. They create new and astonishing worlds, and they are free from the shackles of time.

In respect of your time and efforts to read my books, I will teach you the identity of a Great being, which you might aspire to be, though this aspiration must only be for your own personal growth and not for the status or opinions of anybody else.

Are you ready?

If so, let our journey begin.

WARNING

For the purposes of this book, I describe the majority of people as 'neuro-regular'. This means the people you see, meet, and work with. This also includes those you don't see, such as so-called 'celebrities' or 'stars', a group of people who society decorates using its regular criteria. I don't consider anyone rich or famous to be a star or a Great.

Indeed, the general identity of the homo sapiens species is neuro-regular. Generally, the homo sapiens species have neuro-regular brains. However, there are some humans who have different brain identities. For example, Aspergians like me are not neuro-regular. Therefore, I argue that Aspergians are not homo sapiens, not Earthlings, but a different and advanced species compared to neuro-regulars.

Of course, being neuro-irregular does not make you a Great. You become a Great only by evolving, though someone with a neuro-irregular brain may stand a better chance of evolving because the neuro-regular brain does not even recognise the horror they are living in and the disgusting species of human they are forced to live alongside. The neuro-irregular brain recognises that it is different from the rest of the species.

Note that if someone else calls me a Great or the opposite, I don't care a penny. What anyone has in their own mind is their own business, which I don't care for, nor am I willing to interfere to change their mind. It is only me who can place myself in the category of the Greats.

I hope I am clear and fair on this from the start. However, if you disagree with me on any of my theories or arguments, feel free to argue against me anytime, okay?

However, please do not judge me or my book by your standards. Please never judge any author who has a book in their mind, and who has taken the time to offer it to the world, even if you disagree with its contents or delivery.

So, please consider this a warning and leave now if you are not ready for what you are about to read, or if you are easily offended by threats to your ego or opinions that are different to your own.

Part 1

THE SOCIETIES OF NEURO-REGULARS

History 1:

THE HUMAN LAUNDRY

The first thing you must understand is that the majority of human animals in the world are being laundered into self-perceived important beings from childhood. This is a process that I call 'man laundering' or 'human laundering'. In this history, you will understand why.

The Brain Laundry

From our childhood, we are stuck in the continuous, never-ending process of the brain laundry. In *The Temple of Consciousness*, you learned about the role of family, school, nation, religion, and social media, which demonstrated why you are this specific person and not any other. Now, you will learn about the concept of man laundering, which explains why this happens.

In the foundations of our current civilisation, we are all animals by nature. Do you disagree with me? Listen, we do everything that the other animals on this planet do and we are governed by our instincts... do you disagree with that? Do you rate yourself as superior to the other animals? Undoubtedly, most humans view themselves as better than other animals on this planet.

Why is that? Well, humans have the perception of power and superiority from money or from being in a certain position (such as a religious authority, politician, landowner, multi-millionaire, or multi-billionaire in the current era of power, though the man laundering process applies to all eras of civilisation).

And why is that? Because the authorities want you to believe that you are the ultimate, most important being. From childhood, you are pushed violently to think that you have a purpose: a dream, a family, a career, a job, and a place in the afterlife kingdom of the religions. All of society's institutions and social habits are based on the target to launder your animal nature into a sophisticated form of intelligence. In fact, it's crazy how easily people ignore their original animalistic nature and behave like they are the most dominant beings in the universe.

Do you not believe me? Let's consider the concept of family and marriage, which we will discuss in more depth later. What do you think marriage and family are? They are institutions created by society. This is why when someone says they are married, I feel both sympathy and disdain for them. My disdain is total and non-negotiable, but I have sympathy because I am watching people being forced to waste their own time on something that is ultimately not productive.

What do you think about studies, colleges, universities, degrees, and diplomas? You think that they are positive things, accolades, necessities. Hey moron, you are addicted to the decoration that those in control of society push you towards. In reality, these things mean nothing. They cannot make you superior to any other animal or human animal.

What do you think about jobs and careers? Every day, I see people working with passion and pride thinking they are doing something great! Scientists, yuppies, high-level professionals, workers, technicians, journalists, and TV personalities — all of them living in the illusion that they are important, useful, precious beings[1] — thinking that if they stopped existing, we would cry and consider it such an unfortunate event to happen in our lifetimes.

During the pandemic, I witnessed the spectacular performance of all kinds of specialists who 'explained' the various issues related to Covid-19 to us spectators and I laughed. People always think they are so important to other people. They are convinced that they are vital to our daily routine and that without their advice, we are probably doomed to die! This is why I laugh any time I see someone busy in their 'career' duties.

You see, the man laundering process of turning you into a 'precious' being is never-ending. If you don't believe me, just think how easily you accept the social habits of our particular era.

I see you working every day to secure bread for your family and I see what a happy and proud slave you are.

I see you with a woman or a man walking together on the streets of a Greek or Turkish island.

I see you with your spouse and two kids walking as a family in my city of Limassol.

---

[1] Note that the personal evolution of some individuals during the annals of human history have proved to be sporadic events that by no means make any considerable impact on the general history of the species.

I see you, TV presenter with a sky-high salary, pretending you are a must-watch persona.

I see you, everybody, in your daily routines. I see how deeply your mind is enslaved to the propaganda that you are someone important while you are really just an animal. What a species indeed! What a species to admire.

Do you know what I think of you? That you are a brainwashed slave of the laundering industry of man, an industry that applies the laundering process against you and enslaves your mind so tightly that it's impossible to escape, so tightly that you don't even want to escape from your cosy, little cocoon.

Get lost. I am already above you so I don't mind disclosing to everybody what you really all are. Animals.

Dirty animals who just escaped from the bathroom, leaving the shitty and the dirtiness of their miserable animal nature there. No decoration can change this nature. No diploma, no career, no job, nothing. You are a shitty, dirty animal and my duty is to remind you of your horrible nature at any moment.

If you don't like it, then I recommend that you leave this book now. This book is only for people who want to see the truth.

History 2:

NOAH'S THEORY ON THE HUMAN ANIMAL

In this history, you will find my original theory on this species, homo sapiens. To understand this, we must study where we live, what we understand, and which version of reality we experience. So, let's examine my greatest ever cosmic design for you, the Animal Verse.

A Brief History of Consciousness

The Earth is approximately 4.5 billion years old and intelligent life has occupied it for a very small part of this time. It's estimated that humans have existed for around 6 million years, but those humans were not 'intelligent life' and were almost nothing like the humans we know today. According to archaeologists, humans became homo sapiens, which was an estimated 200,000–300,000 years ago, and we still call them 'modern humans'.

At some time in the history of these modern humans, homo sapiens gained a higher level of consciousness and developed language. Scientists do not agree on why this occurred. According to scientists, the universe was a cosmic event that came from almost nothing, or came from the nearest point to nothing, as they describe the birth conditions of our universe. However, their hypothesis is totally out of logic or at least totally out of my logic. (I decided a long time ago that my logic is not the same level as yours, or anyone else's, because we are not at the same level of evolution and expansion of consciousness.)

In *The Temple of Consciousness*, I attempted to solve this query of creation. In contrast to the scientific hypothesis, I proposed the concept of the Composers. I argued that those in the conscious realms decided to colonise humans' minds with the capacity for consciousness an estimated 70,000 – 100,000 years ago (nobody really knows). During these pre-conscious times, the Composers colonised one animal in the Earth Zoo with consciousness as an experiment on how they would live within the universe. Of course, someone else decided the experiment, not us, the animals. The animals never choose the experiments conducted against them.

Anyhow, the implantation of consciousness was the reason why humans were able to develop language after millions of years of silence and grunting like our fellow animals. This spark led modern humans to develop the first primitive foundations of civilisation, eventually leading to the societies and humans we see around us today. However, the burden of consciousness, the spark implanted in humans, only began to really evolve in the last 10,000–12,000 years, when civilisation start to become more structured.

As such, the evolution of intelligent consciousness has been an extremely slow process and unfortunately, our intelligent evolution was not consistent, meaning it did not include the majority of humans. Most humans stayed the same: very similar to animals, even though they lived in villages, towns, and eventually cities, rather than in the wild like the other animals.

Yet, as a species, we do have a few crucial differences compared to the other animals in the Earth zoo. Animals do not have the same level of consciousness as us, are not evolving in the same way, are not creating civilisations, are not governed by any kind of logic, and do not have advanced forms of language. Of course, other animals have their own primitive 'languages' but we can't understand them, at least so far.

Animals are designed by nature to adjust very successfully to their physical environment or vice versa, an environment can be hostile to every species but one, but this is not the same as developing consciousness. We humans are a colony of animals, but we were selected among the rest of animals as the only species to be privileged to become a colony of *conscious* animals. We were chosen to carry a conscious load in this Animal Verse, the name I baptised this universe with.

We see the way we see and we observe what we observe because we are located in the Animal Verse. We can't see anything outside our area of human animals, though there is far more to see.

The Theory of Shells and Shellies

I discussed this concept, among many others, with my Russian friend here in Limassol called Tatiana. She has lived here for more than 25 years with her family and children. I am a fan of Tatiana. She is my favourite lioness fighter as she never gives up. Any time life behaves unfortunately to her, she immediately stands up with a bright spirit to fight again.

Once, we were talking about the nature of humans and the ugly behaviour of almost every human. She surprised me with the following statement: "what do you think we are as a species? We all carry around 2 kilos of shit at any moment." Essentially, that is a bowling ball's worth of shit. (In fact, some sources estimate up to 9kg.)[i]

For years, I had shared similar thoughts to Tatiana's and boosted by the monumental revelation of her statement, I built Noah's new theory: *that we humans are animals with a dirty, ugly, blasphemous, violent, and greedy nature, producing only shit, both physically and mentally.* In this theory, I propose that every male human animal is called Shell and every female human animal is called Shelly. Why the names Shell and Shelly? Because any human being is just a shell that contains shit, obviously.

Remember that the difference between us and the rest of the animals in the Earth zoo is that apart from being loaded with shit, we also carry the load of consciousness. The downside of this is that the shit is not only physical excrement but also our thoughts and actions. We are all loaded with shit physically in our bodies, but also mentally in our brains. Thus, we can't produce anything more than shit. Physically one to three times a day and mentally at any moment with our thoughts and actions. What a funny species!

The Progression of Shells and Shellies

In this history, I replace the biblical names of Adam and Eve with Shell and Shelly as our forefather and foremother ancestors. Of course, Shell and Shelly were not a single couple as in the case of Adam and Eve, but they represent a large community of ancestors who were colonised in the same period. We all came from a few hundred or a few thousand shell ancestors who were first colonised with the load of consciousness.

Our ancestors, the Shells and Shellies, started very slowly to explore the cosmos. For tens of thousands of years, they learned how to find food, how to survive, and not die. What we see today, what we think we know about science, technology, and the cosmos, has its origin and roots in how our ancestors reacted to the new conscious status steadily through the millennia.

These foundations were and are logic — a brain property we gained as a species from consciousness — and observation. Their tools were and are the 'hands capability' as I call it. Without this specific capability, no civilisation would exist for us. This is civilisation within a colony of animals with a hand capability.

You feel proud of your achievements as a species, don't you? But how long and how far do you think Shells and Shellies can go? Are we near to the end? Are we near our limits and boundaries? How far can a species of Shells go with their shitty nature? Are you kidding me, dear fellow Shell or Shelly? Are you aware of your dirty miserable nature? Or perhaps you think that by wearing glamorous clothes and placing perfume on your body, you hide your dirtiness?

Look beyond you. Do you see any planetary vision of what's happening around us? Do you see any planetary collective systematic effort to stop climate change? Providing of course that climate change is really happening (personally I don't know, but let's take for granted that is happening).

Do you see any planetary vision to stop people leaving their countries to move to rich countries like masses of sheep? Well, there is no vision for any of the major challenges from anybody. What we witness is meaningless meetings in various cities where the 'leaders' of the United Kingdom (UK) and United States of America (USA) pleasantly snore during the talks. Some 'leaders' talk while others snore in their great ambitions to save this planet from climate change. Haha!

As a species, we have not evolved since the homo sapiens Shells and Shellies started to think and observe nature. This is why the developments in technology and science through the various eras of humans (especially in the 20th and 21st century) are enormous yet still primitive. So, never overestimate where we live and what we can do as a species.

We are at the same point of physical evolution as our ancestors were some tens of thousands of years ago! We still have the same needs: energy, water, food, and sex to survive. Therefore, we are still vulnerable to all diseases, including new and even more aggressive ones than before. We are at the power of randomness. We are aging rapidly. We are dirty Shells and Shellies, and we are full of shit inside in our bodies and minds.

So, always remember that our nature is wild, ugly, and dirty because we are animals. Most of the time, our human shells are so ugly and dirty that we don't even need to open them to feel disgust. We are disgusting in our appearance, behaviours, attitudes, and arrogance. And because of this filthy, primitive nature, we are all Shells and Shellies stuck in our cage in the Earth zoo, unable to see past the end of our own noses to what is beyond.

The Known Reality

Our area is the anthropic universe, the universe that we think we watch and explore (for information, anthropic means: *involving or concerning the existence of human life*). However, there are areas outside the anthropic area, beyond our senses.

Reader, never overestimate the power and length of this species' senses. We realise and recognise only what is within the applied area of our senses. Outside of that, we are totally blind and ignorant to the existence of other areas. Some scientists claim that we don't realise the existence of other areas, dimensions, or worlds of space-time (as they call it) because they were separated from us at the time of the universe's genesis, during the so-called Plank era (the very early and extremely short era of the big bang, as the theories claim).

However, do you think that scientists know a lot about the material universe? If you do, I would like to inform you that scientists are just like you. They are copies of your ignorant self. They observe the universe exactly as you observe it, with the anthropic senses within the anthropic area, which is governed by the anthropic laws. And they always see or observe what they have in mind that they must see or observe.

I can prove this statement very easily. Even you, with just your eyes, can see in the cloudy sky any figure, shape, or image you decide on. You may see human figures, animals, or spaceships. You can very easily see anything you wish as a cloud image! The same applies but more strictly for any observer equipped with the latest power of technology and computers. They observe what the scientific theories predict. They observe what they expect to observe. Their minds are not freely observing entities. They are already preoccupied by the predictions of the theories. They never imagine for themselves and it never passes through their minds that the scientific theory might be crap, or just a brain model, or just a small part of the bigger picture, which is unapproachable to the current phase of the technology.

You see, we all live within a specific package of physical laws, but this doesn't mean that there are no other packages of physical laws out there. And just because our package runs smoothly in our area doesn't mean that there aren't other packages that run smoothly in their own areas, nor does it mean they must run the same way as ours.

Yet, because science only focuses on the anthropic areas, all scientific theories about the material universe are primitive, incomplete, and doomed to end, even to be replaced by new anthropic data. This is why science and technology can expand the boundaries of our anthropic observations but they can never drive us outside the observable, anthropic areas.

Do you think that everything out there works only because of us? That it works only in the anthropic way and not in any other way? What the hell do you think our species is, the dominant and sovereign beings of the whole universe? That our reality is the only one?

Our known reality is just a version of reality among many other versions, the latter of which I call the dark reality (as it is dark to us, meaning unknown and unreachable). However, there is always a distinction between the general version and the special version that is the reality of all of us separately. Put more simply, your special reality is not the same as my special reality, so we don't experience or understand the concepts and phenomenon of life in the same way.[2]

You must also understand that there are a lot of grey areas between reality and illusion. For example, why do you think that you really live? Do you actually live or just think that you live? Where are the others who don't live, those who have died, and those who have not been born yet? There are huge numbers of other beings whose existence you don't realise.

Do you understand that empty space is impossible? Accordingly, it doesn't matter that you don't see them; there are far more beings and entities in space considered empty by your senses. Sometimes, you think that you are alone as there are no other humans in the area. But how many others are right next to you, yet you don't see them and they don't see you?

As you can understand, what we think and consider to be reality is just a version of reality, the reality of conscious animals in the universe of the animals. We only have the power to understand this specific version of the universe and our power is backed by the specific package of physical laws that is running.

---

[2] Likewise, one of the greatest properties of my hypothesis is that consciousness is the mother of logic, so it's impossible for there to be a common logic. The so-called common logic is an illusion, a myth, among the massive other illusions and myths that your personal life is stacked with.

The Perception of Superiority

Unfortunately, most of our fellow species find it extremely difficult to accept that they only live in and explore their own version of reality, and that theirs is a very small part of reality within the vast areas of the entire dark reality. Likewise, it is extremely difficult for our fellow species to accept that there are other forms of intelligence apart from the colonised animal's one, which is their own.

Here, my thesis is strong and backed by concrete evidence. Simply look around you at the rest of the animals. Look at your pets or any other animal. Look at a field full of cows while they are eating and place yourself next to them. What do you think? You think that they are a lower form of intelligence than you, correct? So, who are you, the top form of intelligence? The sovereign and dominant form of intelligence? The king of the intelligence?

Hey moron, if there is a form that is certainly lower than you, then it's undoubtable that there are forms higher than you, correct? Of course, there are higher beings and Supreme Beings, those who watch you. You are simply an animal colonised by a conscious load and you are merely participating in a cosmic experiment on how animals are watching the animal version of their universe.

If the universe has many other versions, many other version realities, many other parcels of reality according to their equivalent package of physical laws, then do you understand how minor you are even if you can consciously think about your important self? Important to who and for whom? To the other animals like you? What a joke!

This is the human animal's primitive, vulnerable, mortal, shitty nature. It is mortal because most humans are not qualified to gain the brain property of non-mortal status. So, for this animal, it's impossible to survive or explore the vast number of parcels of physical laws. The human animal explores only the anthropic parcel of laws and observes only the animal anthropic edition of this parcel of the universe, the Animal Verse.

History 3:

THE SEARCH FOR ALIEN LIFE

Now you understand the Animal Verse more, I will I explain the concept of aliens and why you will never meet or discover any alien person, visitor, or civilisation, and why our scientists are living in a giant illusion in their search for alien civilisations.

The Fruitless Search

My first question to you, reader, is can we Earthling animals travel in space? The answer is obviously no. Not now, not after a million years, never. How far could you travel in space 'equipped' with your physical body? You are not programmed, dear loser, to escape the Animal Verse or the animal planetary solar system. It is a forbidden dream for you. You are just an animal running in the experiment called: how the animals are watching the universe. OK? So far, so good.

Second question, check your fucking physical body, dear and tell me: can you travel at the speed of light? Or can you travel even near to the speed of light as a physical object, as a space passenger? Of course not. Why? I remind you of the nature of your body. Not only is it technologically not possible, but it is physically impossible for you! We are forced by the applied laws of nature.

Still, there is no need to use your imagination to consider how a spaceship could travel at such high speeds like the speed of light. Hey, how can you travel in space at such astronomical distances when you need an hour to drive five miles in busy traffic? Haha! We humans are doomed to live here and die here as physical bodies.

Secondly, even if we could travel in space, it would be totally useless and we would only find more morons like us out there. Are the laws of nature, the known package of laws, running everywhere and in obligatory uniformity in the whole Animal Verse? The answer is obviously yes. Then why would somewhere else in the animal universe, the version of the universe we observe, be different than us? It is impossible for any other form of intelligence out there to be anything else than us, OK? Do you realise that?

I remember when I was a child, I thought that by going to other countries, I could meet different people. Haha, what a cute child's worry! Later in life, I discovered that people are the same everywhere: dirty, vulnerable, stupid, violent, selfish, greedy, and arrogant, and this is applied across all of the species by their limited capacity of learning and evolving. Everywhere I go, I just meet Shells and Shellies.

And you, Mr Scientist, are just like me as a child. What you are searching for is Shells and Shellies in exoplanets similar to Earth, with inhabitants exactly like you, your wife, and exactly like your ugly neighbour. So why do you expect something different from yourself?

Look dear scientist, nobody is out there to find. Nobody different than you and your ugly neighbour. Is that clear? The observable version of the universe, the Animal Verse, is probably full of more fools like you. Those fools are doomed to stay there on their planet, to observe the same version that you observe. They are doomed and cursed to never escape to other planets or receive visits from other planets.

The morons, like Earthlings, can't reach you by any means and you can't reach them either. Morons are genetically designed and doomed to live separately and isolated from each other. They have the same fate and destiny to the one you have my dear fool. Please bear in mind this colossal and powerful new knowledge; there isn't anyone out there more advanced than you to find, OK?

There aren't any advanced or more advanced beings than your primitive selves out there to discover you. You are both living in the animal universe. You are both living within the boundaries of the same package of physical laws, which apply universally to the specific version of the Animal Verse that you both observe and watch, OK?

According to my theory, there will be no one here to colonise another planet, no one out there in the Animal Verse to discover us because there is no one more technologically advanced than us. They all reach their highest potential and then they fall down and this has probably happened to countless civilisations before us in the Animal Verse.

Anyone alive now in the Animal Verse apart from us is either at the top of their potential as we are, or behind us in our various time-points of civilisation. Perhaps somewhere a man called Jesus has just been born, somewhere a queen called Hatshepsut is ruling the Egypt as a female king, and somewhere people are living in the 1970s or 1980s, which were my favourite decades.

You see, you think that you explore the universe but please understand that what you see and what you explore is just one edition, one version, of the universe: the animal edition. And there are an enormous number of editions depending on the package of physical laws that apply and depending on each individual's parcel of reality.

Who told you that there is only one edition of the universe? Who told you that there is only one package of physical laws? Who told you that there is only one parcel of reality and that this one is yours! Do you believe them? What a moron you are, my dear!

Have you ever thought that to travel in space, you need to get rid of your physical body? Do you want to carry your useless body with you? If yes, then this is my evidence that you are doomed to die here, without any realistic chance of colonising another planet ever! Not in 200 years, not in 2 million years, if you remain stuck in your physical body.

So, start to think differently. Start to think that it's possible to abandon your physical body and still be a conscious being or entity. And don't bother chasing an illusionary future of colonising another planet. You have no future at all! You are at the end of the road. The experiment is near to finishing. You and your species have already destroyed a large part of the planet's flora and fauna. And now, you are doomed to be stuck here on this decaying planet, dear friend.

We are merely Shells and Shellies, stuck here in our shitty shells.

Bodiless Intelligence

Instead, can you imagine how we would have formed as a species if we had been colonised by consciousness yet forced to start the exploration of the cosmos without this hands capability? It's unthinkable, isn't it? For me, however, it is very well thinkable. In fact, it was the reason for building my brand-new perception of the cosmos, which is a postmodern model of perception with zero relationship to or connection with everything you know so far.

Ask yourself, if there is a higher form, an evolved one compared to you, they must have a different shape to you, mustn't they, like the difference in shape between you and a cow? They must not have a shitty shape obviously. No fucking digestive system, right? Perhaps a shapeless form of intelligence? A bodiless one? One formed of pure energy? Or maybe one that chose a shape? One that can take any shape necessary to invade your version of reality? To travel outside the dark reality to meet you in this version where you live as a prisoner?

Can you imagine a form of intelligence that is of pure energy? An advanced form of bodiless intelligence that is handless? Why can't you? Can't you imagine an intelligent bodiless being, a being that exists without any physical body?

A bodiless form means that such entities are free from pooping and peeing every day or several times every day. A bodiless entity is handless. Such forms do everything without any physical touch, by just ordering and just making it happen.

Those who have bodiless intelligence have other advanced capacities too. For them, all physical affairs caused by a specific package of laws or the known ordinary laws simply do not exist. No illnesses, no aging, no suffering from any kinds of physical violence. No need to fight to secure food, water, or any other essential — to us — life sources.

Of course, the core advantage, the greatest of all trophies, is the neutralisation of feelings and emotions, with the exception of creative peace. A bodiless form of intelligence is an advanced one compared to your misery. A pure energy form, that lives in the dark figurative reality where you cannot access. An advanced form that may abandon the areas of the dark reality at any time to visit you in your version of reality. An advanced form of intelligence living within advanced natural laws and evolved matter.

The concept of evolved matter is the pair of the known matter and evolved matter is composed of smart particles. This means that the bodiless form of intelligence may travel from the dark reality to yours taking on any physical shape known to us, be it man, woman, young, old… whatever form they want to have fun with and conduct experiments against you. At any moment in your life, an 'alien' may be next to you but because they look human, you will never realise their original nature.

So, please, morons of Earth, stop seeking 'alien' civilisations and accept your fate as fallible, physical beings, as Shells and Shellies with your 2kg of shit, doomed to die here on this planet in this primitive Animal Verse.

History 4:

THE CONSCIOUSNESS OF ARTIFICIAL INTELLIGENCE

In the last history, we considered the prospect of alien life. In this history, we will consider the prospect of artificial intelligence (AI).

The Development of AI

Let me start with a question: why am I here as an author and you as a reader? Because we both carry a load of consciousness and because of this unique privilege in the Animal Verse, we have developed language, logic, and so many wonderful applications of them. And based on those foundations, we have built the current civilisation, which is a very ugly, dirty, and unviable one, but still a civilisation with all of us as contributors.

Among our other achievements, there is a lot of talk in our era about the creation of artificial intelligence, a creation of the human animal that some humans believe will take us over. Many people ask, "is there any chance for machines with AI to develop consciousness?" Some people, Elon Musk included, believe that we can't exclude such a scenario. Of course, he can't prove it. Nobody can prove such a claim.

Indeed, nobody can prove the origin of consciousness because nobody really knows. (I have my own theory, which is explained in detail in *The Temple of Consciousness*.) The current human animal hypothesis is: consciousness is a physical process that emerges from the complexity of the neurons' interactions in the brain. However, this remains a hypothesis or simply an opinion without any evidence.

All of my foundations and discoveries about the origin of consciousness totally and absolutely exclude the probability of a conscious machine one day becoming the human animal's governor. Put more simply, there will be never any conscious machine, either smart, intelligent, or stupid. There will always just be machines.

Why? Because, remember that according to my models, consciousness is not an Earthling product or a biological procedure. It is colonisation of our brain from higher sources. So, no machine created by humans may develop consciousness because we are not the owners of consciousness to bestow it upon others. We are already governed by consciousness, so how can we become creators of consciousness?

This is why any smart machine or AI will always remain a machine, not a conscious being. On the contrary, we are already living in the era of smart machines. Why? Because we created a new generation of humans who work and behave not as naturally intelligent beings but as programmed intelligent machines. Indeed, the societies of neuro-regulars are themselves becoming smart machines, talking machines, thinking machines, working machines. I have seen this myself.

Recently, I was in a busy bar. On the large TV screens, there was a live Premier League football match between Tottenham and Newcastle. I started to watch it. As time passed, the match proved to be very interesting to my eyes. Not because of the football, of course. The story was the players' behaviour. I was not watching humans but artificial intelligence machines fighting on the pitch.

Just look at them. Are they humans? C'mon fellas! They're not. They are programmed, highly paid machines to 'entertain' the societies of neuro-regulars as football stars. Haha! The funny thing is that all of those machines are 'idols' for the children of the neuro-regulars! The children are in love with the machines. What a massive downgrade for this species indeed.

So, don't bother me again about AI. It is already here and it is already a sad fact. The humans are the AI, not the machines. The humans have already been downgraded to behave as machines.

However, the fact that humans are losing their share of the total intelligence of the planet does not necessarily mean that any other form of intelligence will gain a profit and therefore replace humans as the next governor of intelligence on Earth. On the contrary, the issue is that the human species is going down fast and the vast majority of humans are nothing more than working machines.

While there is massive technological and scientific progress, the evolution and expansion of intelligence is at its lowest level. You see, science and technology are moving quickly forwards, while humanity is rapidly moving backwards in terms of intelligence. Parallel worlds!

This is why there is a danger that smart machines or smart robots will replace many people in vast numbers, which is a big and real threat for people who work hard to secure bread and milk for their families. You are no more than a working machine, my friend, and soon you will have no use, no meaning for the job or labour market.

Why would a company employee you and not hire or buy some smart machine to do the job instead of you? Can you imagine that? Can you imagine that your hands, your mind, and your power will be replaced by smart machines? How can you, or anyone, or any government cope with this tremendous and colossal change of working hands? Well, this has already started happening in factories, in supermarkets with self-checkouts, and with online ordering systems.

What horrible conclusion arises? That billions of human working machines will one day soon be absolutely useless because smart machines will replace them. This is the danger, not any other ridiculous notion that AI will prevail against conscious intelligence. Instead, the reality is that humans are the losers of the 21st century because they stopped evolving.

The Smart Sheep

So, humans stopped evolving… but not only that, I see the younger generations behaving, acting, and realising the phenomenon of life not as conscious beings but rather as smart machines. More specifically, like smart masses of sheep.

This is the reason why I hate social media so much — because it is flooded with smart sheep. Don't be misled by the fact that famous people and even politicians use social media. What are they by themselves other than smart sheep?

My lesson to you is never be misled by anyone who presents themselves as 'important', famous, an expert, or an idol. They are all Shells and Shellies, and they all contain shit in their miserable bodies and minds. Every morning when you go to work, think of the people you work with as animals in shells who just got rid of their shit in their bathroom, or gleefully shared them with you in the workplace bathroom.

One smart sheep sent me this email:

Hey Noah!

Social media — you either love it or hate it.

If it's the latter, chances are that you may not understand how to use it effectively as an author.

But with over 3.9 billion people using social media in 2022, it's transforming the way people find information, buy products (like books!), and connect with others — so you can't afford to ignore it!

You want to leverage social media to grow your author platform, but how do you actually promote your book without feeling inauthentic, or sales-y?

My reply to that email was: "Who the hell told you that I care what 3.9 billion sheep are doing? Who the hell told you that I have anything in common with these masses of expendable people?" Just fuck off, all of you. The social media of the neuro-regulars is not in my area of interest. I know who they are. I know that they are neuro-regulars. I don't need lessons from any neuro-regular on how to live with neuro-regulars, OK?

I am scared to think what would happen if any one of those neuro-regulars happened to open my book! What would they understand of the content? One word or two at the most? Do you really believe that I write my books for these people? If so, what a moron you are!

As a financially free man, a being of great consciousness, why would I need to downgrade myself so badly just to meet the level of smart sheep? A higher being never gives a penny about what a lesser being is doing, remember. And as a conscious being, I strongly argue that no machine, either smart or stupid, will capture or conquer me in the future. Enough from you smart sheep.

History 5:

THE HUMAN SEXUAL ANIMAL

Despite us living in the latter days of this civilisation (which may last for decades, but is certainly the latter days), humans continue to reproduce at increasing rates. In this history of the human sexual animal, you will discover why.

The Institution of Marriage

Hey reader, who told you that marriage, families, and having children are good? Have you ever considered that the human animal is the only animal with the consciousness to know better than continually reproducing and flooding our planet with too many people… yet it has the stupidity to keep doing so?

For most people, marriage is not in our human animal nature. I argue that we are largely polygamous as a species and that we cannot violently go against our nature, just like many animals in the Animal Verse. I argue that our original nature demands a change in sex partners and that we cannot exist with any regular sex partner.

Scientists are still debating this subject, but the current consensus is that very early humans (pre-religion) developed to become monogamous when humans became centred around families rather than tribes. In other words, the basic human animal is biologically designed to reproduce and at some point, realised that being monogamous generally resulted in the production of stronger, healthier, and generally better offspring.[ii]

As such, many human animals developed a genetic trait that made them swans rather than apes, like we were originally. This why some humans tend to, or wish to, mate for life like swans because they have a strong genetic background to do so.[iii]

You must understand that the human behaviours you see today have their roots in the circumstances that our ancestors experienced through the millennia. In many cases, this resulted from the way that they were violently, mentally, or societally forced to behave in a specific way. In other words, their conditioning.

Consider this: why do certain people have predetermined cardiac genetic factors that mean they will develop heart failure? Why do some women have the genetic factor to develop breast cancer or men to develop testicular cancer? So, why do some humans have the predetermined genetic factor to develop life-mate relationships like swans? Because of the way their ancestors lived and the genes they passed on.

For millennia, humans' social habits forced people to mate for life because of their strong desire to have children and create families. Then, various religions forced people to get married to create more children and families, and therefore to enlarge the member base of that religion. For some humans, these factors created the genetic trait of being swans, while many others remain in their original ape-like state of polygamy.

There are many married couples, far more than you can imagine, who agree with me, not only as a theoretical principle but because of their personal, physical realisation. Some even have a separate sexual life with younger partners, and by this I don't mean a relationship but casual sex.

However, like almost anything in the Animal Verse, some humans found a way to capitalise on this genetic trait. That is why there is a huge factory selling bullshit built on the foundation of family and supposed 'love stories' between mates. From Hollywood, to the publishing industry, to Christmas, just to mention few of the bullshit factories.

There are mountains of best-selling Hollywood films, books, and music songs all about love stories. Billions of dollars are circulating and the owners of the entertainment industry are making astronomical profits by selling these love stories to the societies of the neuro-regulars.

Hey, I don't care about your love story, OK? Your story is a meaningless detail in the ocean of events. I don't care for anyone's individual story, just as I don't care how the ancient Egyptian queens cleaned their anuses after pooping in the ancient toilets in front of their female slaves. It is all irrelevant to me.

The Connection of Boxes

Why don't I care about these things? Because marriage and family are big time-wasting factors that go against our personal evolution. I have evidence: I see family people after 20 years and nothing has changed for them. They remain stuck, as if not even a second separates them from our last meeting 20 years ago! The only obvious difference is the aging of their shell, but nothing else! Otherwise, they have the same stupid faces, the same stupid attitude, even the same stupid discussions. That's why I leave them to 'enjoy' their miserable families.

Me, I am forever single. What I need is a housemaid and I have one. I live with my beloved Joti, my domestic helper. It is unthinkable for me to live in the same house as a lover or spouse, or indeed to take one. I feel superior to everyone who lives within marriage and families. Nobody in a marriage can judge me for criticising marriage and the creation of family, so shut up and read. No one will hear or care for your shouting apart from your spouse.

Personally, I am not willing to abandon my evolutionary process for the 'enjoyment' of a family. I am totally devoted to evolving and I have no time to waste 'investing' in a sure-loser horse, which marriage and family both are.

Aside from the case of happy swans, marriage and family are both giant illusions. Why be with this man or woman but not with any other? Why must I be with somebody and not with nobody? Why do I exist? Why must this fucking civilisation continue to exist and not collapse, making a huge noise on its way down?

Sometimes, when I post or talk about my beliefs on marriage, people reply that if everyone shared my crazy ideas, then no one would be here to listen to or read them. This is not my problem. If our society is full of neuro-regulars, it's not my problem.

Other people ask me, "hey Noah, do you never want to have sex?" Of course, I don't give a penny about people's opinions or silly questions. People are innocent and naïve, and are still in the phase of zero-evolution. They remain the same as their ancient ancestors. Nothing has changed during the last millennia concerning this species' evolution.

If I reply that I am sexually neutral, that I hate the human body because it is meat together with fat, they think I am alien who has neutral sexuality amongst common Earthlings. However, sex has importance and probably great importance when it takes place within certain humans, as you will see in the next history.

The Net of Illusions

Imagine how human relations start for normal people like you. You meet a man or woman by the force of randomness and your mind is already trapped in the nets of illusions. You never take into account the myriad of unsolved boxes, you never connect the moments, you never connect the current present with the future present.

Do you know if this man or woman is a criminal-minded? A psychopath? Do you know if they are hiding dangerous habits such as jealousy, gambling, alcohol, or drugs? Do you know if they will consider you as a pet and property during the unavoidable routine of a boring marriage?

Do you understand, my dear lady, that the vast majority of men will look out of the marriage to gain new and fresh sexual experiences? What did you say, that your man is the exception? That your man is a swan who never looks at other women? Haha, you are so funny my dear! However, I hope you find a true swan because a small percentage of men are swans indeed. Unfortunately for you, most men do not behave like swans. They are sex hunters forever. And sex for this kind of man is not with their wife. Sex for this kind of man always means new experiences.

Some people claim that they are very happily married because they receive pure interest, love, and friendship from their partners, no matter what the sexual relationship is like between them. Personally, I have never tried this and I have never been involved in a marriage, but I hear it from a lot of ordinary couples, especially the elderly ones, and I understand and accept such claims as original and genuine. Perhaps the men in these relationships are swans.

Don't worry… if you don't find a swan, I have developed the application of professional mothers. Women can choose perfectly from a sperm bank for the purpose of creating children. They can take care of them until the age of 18 and get support from the state for their salary, school, and monthly expenses, and they may choose to have separate personal sex relations with men. What a wonderful application to maintain this 'wonderful' species of homo sapiens. Now I am crying from happiness!

The Alternative to the Family

You see, we can find an alternative to family creation through other smart methods. We live in a smart era, or in the smart-fake era, of AI, remember? Although this smart era will be short if we don't change our attitude, there is always the hope that we will avoid the self-destruction of our current civilisation. We may be the first ever in the history of the universe to evolve and achieve this.

Here, I remind you of my prediction that we have only a few years remaining before the collapse of civilisation. According to my observations and models, this civilisation has less than 30 years — as I stated in *The Temple of Consciousness* — and less than 10 years in my updated prediction in *The Animal Verse*. These predictions are not Nostradamus predictions; I am not Nostradamus. My predictions are based on my observations and well-backed evidential models.

The difference in my prediction from 30 down to 10 years is due to the new events of the war in Ukraine, recession, the fast acceleration rate of immigration from poor to rich countries, the new pandemics predicted to appear because of overpopulation, and the easy movement of virus-carriers across the world.

However, this time limit of 10–30 years is by no means the end, OK? What it means is that huge structural change must occur by changing the attitudes of the world's wealth owners. If this applies to the current flow of events globally, then civilisation can continue. If there is no change at all, then the end will be our self-designed catastrophe and the dying process of our civilisation may last for decades! A ghost civilisation may last for many decades. Some scientists claim that the dying process of this universe will last forever.

In short, why worry about creating more humans when our civilisation is most likely doomed?

History 6:

THE SEXUAL HOLOCAUST

In the previous history, we looked at the human sexual animal and I said that sex has importance. According to my evidence, this is because of an exotic energy called bioelectric energy (BEE), the most rare and precious form of energy in the universe. In this history, you will learn about it and my discovery of it during the horrific sexual holocaust.

The Theory of BEE

Reader, you are a physical body loaded or surrounded by BEE. When you are young (at least, 18 years old)[3], your BEE is so strong, bright, and touchable! It is like a diamond of brightness surrounding your physical body. The importance of having sex is found in the transformation of BEE from the younger to the older partner through poles (though this doesn't mean that within couples of a similar age, BEE transformation is not possible).

Why is it so powerful within younger to older partners? Well, I must remind you that nothing works as well after a certain age. For example, you can't donate blood to your fellow humans after the age of 75. In the case of BEE, the age limit is much lower. In my opinion, nothing works after the age of

---

[3] Here, I express my strong opposition to many countries that set the legal sex age as anything less 18 years, which encourages official and legal paedophilia in societies.

40. Do you think that you are forever young and loaded with energy? No chance! The age of 40 is far, far away from the age of 25. So, be smart and think smart to find solutions to your aging! Of course, this does not mean that the older person has nothing to attract the younger person with. The energy from the older partner comes from the brightness of their mature brain and the brightness of their money in many cases.

The benefits of receiving BEE from your partner are enormous. This energy boosts your immune system, gives you freshness and youthfulness, gives you more years of active and productive life, and prepares the existence of yourself after you abandon your body! It ensures that you will continue to exist after the death of your physical body. (The destination of your new self is something you will decide and is always relative to your evolutionary status. Don't worry if you evolve day after day, but you should worry if you remain stuck in the Animal Verse.) Unfortunately, most people totally ignore the existence and value of BEE. For ordinary people, their sex life is just pure and animalistic.

The good news is that you never lose any quantity of BEE when you offer it to your partner. You never lose blood when you donate it to your fellow humans, correct? The point is to be in love with the transformation process, no matter whether you love your sexual partner or not. To love the process means taking maximum care for your partner. Never harm your partner through violent sexual behaviour because the partner becomes a victim, a zombie, and loses their BEE (as happens in the sex trafficking industry, which we will move on to shortly).

For women, the best way to reach their BEE is to cover the body of the man with her hands at the peak of her orgasm. For men, the best way is to place their cheek on the cheek of the partner at the peak of his orgasm. The woman must always finish first and the man second. Never together. Why? The BEE exchange works excellently through this method. It is the natural choice for the woman to finish first and man after.

The human body is a monopole, or a wholepole if you will, which are not found anywhere in nature. However, there is no need to search for the pole of the human body to transmit BEE. You simply feel it anywhere you touch the human body – you feel the existence of the energy, for example, by touching the legs. And vice versa, my hand works perfectly as a pole, as do my cheeks, my legs, and all parts of my body because it is a monopole.

According to my experiences, this kind of energy has a birth and death. In the scale of the universe, the energy is applied as a fundamental event in the universe. It applies to all physical bodies of the human species, all other physical species of this planet of animals, and to any other species on any other planet where people and animals like us are living.

Although there is not any scientific evidence backing my thesis, I strongly reject short-sighted science in many cases and not only in this one. I personally discovered this rare and exotic form of energy after I had been involved in the sexual holocaust in south Cyprus, a horrible history in the horizon of events within the Animal Verse.

The Artists of the South Cypriot Sexual Holocaust

When I was fool like you, living only for sex and material delights, I used to be a buyer of women trafficking. Don't rush to call me a fucking bastard. It was **not** like that. The bastard was the country I was living in, south Cyprus. Women trafficking was a national product of this fucking country. By that, I mean it was officially organised by the state, the police, and the authorities. Everything was covered by the legal veil of the south Cyprus regime.

The victims will remain in the history of this holocaust as 'the artists' because this was the identity and title that the regime assigned to give them working permission. *Artists*. This phenomenon lasted for two decades, between 1990–2010, when all cabarets, which were the nests of trafficking these artists, were closed by the local authorities under huge pressure from various international institutes including the EE, UN, and the American Ministry of Foreign Affairs.

Back then, I started as an idiot customer or as the cabaret owners called us, the buyers. Remember, I was like you during those dark periods or to clarify, I was you in the present. Myself in the past is you in the present because I was lacking a basic spiritual education. I was a common idiot of the present times, but in the past.

Initially, I had the feeling that I was in paradise. I experienced very strong and powerful BEE from these young women, who ranged between 18–25 years old. Almost all of the women were innocent village girls from Eastern Europe, Russia, Ukraine, Moldova, Belarus, and other countries like the Philippines, Brazil, and Morocco. Out of all of them, the

Moroccan women had the best mental attitude and were the most intelligent women I ever met in my sexual holocaust life. Of course, I now totally reject any relationship with any woman in the world, so this has no importance or value in my current everyday life.

The victims were massively and hellishly misled by the men or women in their countries acting as agents, promising them very good and highly paid jobs in Western countries. A network of bastards, promising these destitute girls work overseas where they would make a lot of money and help themselves and their families breathe financially.

They were promised dream jobs in a dignified environment and the girls were convinced because they had no defence, no contact with the outside world, no information. They had only heard from rumours that the Western world was a paradise compared to what they were experiencing in their own countries. The result was that they were locked up in the sexual holocaust, one of the greatest unpunished crimes to date against humanity.

Upon arrival in the Western countries, they experienced the first psychological and physical rape. Their passport was confiscated and they had to work to pay for their transport costs. They were then placed in groups in poor housing, with a guard outside to stop those who dared to flee.

From the first evening, they were thrown into the lion's den. They were transported for 'work' to sleazy bars where every bastard of society, every hideous Satan, bought the merchandise of flesh to have it under his sexual authority for the rest of the night. Every bastard of society and white-collar scoundrel had women under their full sexual possession to humiliate, torture sexually, and torture psychologically with cruel behaviour.

Many were offered as a gift to night watchers who were selling protection, as well as police officers to have the police locked and trapped in their fraudulent plans. Always keep in mind, dear reader, that the battles between the mafia groups of the underworld never stopped even for a single second. And mafia groups with the law support of the authorities made tons of money by selling young village women. Imagine a young village girl in a foreign country, who doesn't speak English, and her passport is held by the agents. What kind of defence she could apply?

At the time, south Cyprus was an international bestselling trafficker. Among the population of customers, a large percentage were foreigners living in south Cyprus, sex tourists from various countries and soldiers from the British army base at Akrotiri. The population of customers were internationally barbaric from all around the globe. There were no boundaries, no nationalities, no ages. And all of them showed zero respect for the victims.

I will give you just one example of the myriads I could write about how women trying to seek a better life became victims. I once met a woman from the Dominican Republic who was cheated by those in her country who said that she was going to work as waitress in Spain. The first day we met she was surprised that I wasn't speaking Spanish because she was convinced by the agent and cabaret owner that south Cyprus is a Spanish territory.

The Discovery of BEE

This is how the trafficking of human beings 'worked' at the time, with the victims of the sexual holocaust being many thousands of young women. For these women, the feeling was overwhelming and absolute. Their dreams of decent work that would free them from poverty crumbled. The realisation of deception in such a hideous way caused them immeasurable and inconsolable pain. The sexual violence against the victims was sky high and this was how I accidentally discovered BEE.

For reasons unknown to me, the cabaret owners were sending me all the newly arrived victims. I noticed that two months after each woman's arrival, her BEE was gone. I realised I was touching a cotton-like material and not the skin of a young woman. The reason for this, of course, was the sexual abuse by buyers, one after the other, and often more than once per day because they were forced to offer sex during the afternoon as well as the night.

Animal men were systematically and violently abusing them, so in a period of a few weeks to a few months, they were transformed from dawn flowers, full of freshness and energy, to a dull cotton material as their BEE was plundered by many hungry and barbaric older men. They were carrying serious psychological traumas caused by the customers' sexual behaviour.

Around this time, I also realised that around 10% of the cabaret victims were professional sex businesswomen who used trafficking to increase their business. For me, it was easy to realise this in the first 2 minutes of meeting them. The professionals smoked, spoke good English, always asked for more money, and always asked for a condom. And they had a cotton-like material already! Realising this and living alongside victims of the sexual holocaust, I went to bed with professionals only. I supported the victims in my own way, offering lunches and dinners, buying clothes and shoes for them.

Some of the victims asked me to have sex with them without using a condom, simply as a couple in love. Some suggested marrying me as their only way to escape from the hell of the holocaust. But even during those dark times, I was against marriage, family life, and creating children as a strong personal belief, and therefore I refused all proposals of marriage.

Don't doubt my or their intentions here. Bear in mind that I was a young, gentle, generous, kind, and handsome man. I wasn't committing any crime, as visiting cabarets was legal. Just think how the victims compared me with their population of customers. Imagine how many drunk customers, how many dirty older men, how many violent animals were 'buying' the victims without asking their 'permission'. Imagine how often they were offered for free as gifts to gangsters of the underworld or corrupt police officers.

The Outcome of the Sexual Holocaust

Some of the victims got addicted to the money that came from the job and were repeatedly coming to 'work'. Some got addicted to alcohol in their desperate fight to survive the hell they were forced to live in. Some started as victims but continued as traffickers in their home countries in cooperation with the cabaret owners and agents. Some married customers and had families. Some got divorced.

Many others, almost all actually, developed sexual relationships with the other women-victims there in response to the humiliation from the abominable species called 'men'. They became forced lesbians, as I call them, in their few private moments. Everybody I met confirmed this event. In the eyes of victims of such crime, men are the worst, the most violent, and the most barbaric species to ever appear on Earth. I share the same opinion.

That is why I abandoned trafficking to its own fate in 2005. I was disgusted by what I had witnessed for a decade and I was a rejecter of the human male species. I will hate males forever and no one can change my attitude on that. I was so upset and angry at the authorities of the south Cyprus regime[4] that I couldn't afford to spend any more time there. But listen reader, everywhere in the world there are large trafficking women cartels. All of them are illegal, as illegal as the drug trade. In this case, the sexual holocaust on the island was legally organised by the authorities; the state was the trafficker.

The sexual holocaust is a prime example of how to misuse the transmission of BEE from one body to another. What happened in the sexual holocaust was not a gentle exchange of BEE between couples, but a systematic plundering of BEE by men using sexual violence against young women. Until the end of their lives, these victims will remain scarred by

---

[4] *If you wish to go against the south Cyprus regime, please call me to support you. That would be my greatest pleasure ever. Later, you will learn more about the awful regime that is south Cyprus.*

their experiences. Because of the early, violent loss of their BEE, they will suffer consequences and none of us can predict the size of the consequences for their physical and mental health.

Based on my personal experience, I would suggest that all levels of secondary education in public and in private schools should include lessons on the consequences of sexual violence and teach the young generation about gentle sexual behaviour, which is an essential capacity for anyone who wishes to be placed in the category of civilised humans.

The Hungry Male Eye

From this horrible experience and many other facts and observations, my conclusion is that females are a different species than males. I am sorry dear female readers; I love and admire your nature but the truth is that the male species doesn't. For ordinary males, not for me, you are just a sexual tool. Everywhere you go, a hungry male eye is watching you with the desire to fuck you.

No matter whether you realise it or not, this is the way all males think about females, providing they think you are young and beautiful. You must understand that the vast majority of human males are just filthy animals who want to fuck you and many other women in the Animal Verse. For neuro-regular men, sex always means hunting the rich and bright BEE, without realising what BEE is.

By contrast, how complicated is it for a woman to find a sexual partner in the Animal Verse? Any sexual relationship with men includes obvious risks and dangers because of simple human biology. Men may use sexuality as a weapon against women.

This why being born as a woman is a curse in the Animal Verse. I am very sorry to have to write this kind of statement, but at the same time, I can't pretend that the Animal Verse is beautiful place for women to live. Most women would not share such sentiments or consider themselves or women in general to be vulnerable. However, every day, the media tells us about the rape, kidnap, or murder of women of all ages, and that includes children. Their aggressors are either criminals unknown to them or criminals very well known to them.

The facts are there for everybody to observe. Consider how 47,000 women across the globe were killed by their current partner, ex-partner, or a male family member in 2020. That is every 11 minutes.[iv] When these facts are cited, some men are quick to point out that men are the victims in 80% of all murder cases across the globe. However, they are less quick to mention that the perpetrators are almost always men.

Consider how an estimated 1 in 4 women have been raped or sexually assaulted as an adult, and how half of those rapes are committed by their partner or ex-partner. Again, 98% of those committing sexual offences are men.[v] What else do I need as evidence?

This is why women must be very careful when walking alone and be very wary of strangers. It is also why they should be careful at home and even more wary of the men they know well. All women should be aware that danger is there. Never get inside a stranger's car or go back to man's house who you just met in a bar. You are doomed if you are so naïve. Of course, I'm not saying that all men are monsters, but you have to be exceptionally selective and careful to avoid danger because almost every woman has a story of being sexually assaulted, emotionally assaulted, or raped by a man.

To be born in the Animal Verse as a female? Thanks, but no thanks. I am sorry for that and for what the women of this species must often endure.

History 7:

THE CREATOR OF NEW WORLDS

In this history, I will explain my neutral but not absent sexual life, which is an alternative to the human sexual animal's relations.

Regular People Ruled by Social Habits

Before we begin, understand that I am evolved compared to you and I decided that neutralisation can apply to sex behaviour very well. I am neutral, meaning I do not engage in any sexual relations with any partner, either permanent or temporary.

Since I am a sexually neutral being but at the same time a human in nature, I am not totally alien, so I have performed some experiments in my sex life. These experiments are something you may have never heard of before, but you may never have heard many of the concepts in this book, including the Animal Verse itself. Maybe you have even forgotten that you are an animal.

I guarantee to you that being neutral is something fantastic, something of extraordinary beauty, something astonishing. However, I don't ask anyone to follow me because it's impossible for common people to overcome their physical nature. To achieve such a miracle, the triumph of being a sexually neutral being, I have spent decades and decades investigating and researching the nature of the physical body and all physical phenomena, as well the nature of consciousness.

Nobody really understands the mechanisms behind our 'dream life' or the sleep life of our species. Maybe even you sometimes wonder what the hell dreams are and why during sleep do you feel conscious sometimes? Scientists always have 'solutions' for everything, but they don't really understand a lot of our brain's activities in either the awaking phase or the sleeping phase. This is why I conduct my own experiments.

First, you must understand that I am not a sheep who can sleep straight for eight hours. I wake up very early in the morning, between two and four o'clock, and I practice an aggressive form of meditation for at least an hour or two. After, I decide where I will travel during my upcoming sleep. I order my brain where to deliver me, in which countries, and who I will meet.

Some people call this brain capacity 'lucid dreaming', something that science accepts is possible, though the path that leads to such a monumental experience is uncertain and unknown to science. During my sleep, I realise and recognise the status that I am sleeping but not awake. Maybe you have also sometimes realised that you are sleeping and what you are experiencing is just a dream?

In this state, my main target is to keep my brain conscious while asleep, as I feel that I am gaining conscious time compared to ordinary people. Feeling conscious during your sleep is magical. However, this is the most difficult, complicated, and unthinkable battle of the homo sapiens species. I am just at the beginning of the battle and I already have some good results but I am only inches ahead of the starting line. Practice and patience are my two powerful and efficient weapons to achieve results. Yet, I must clarify that I don't do this every night, and I'm not successful every time.

I also strongly believe that not all people can achieve lucid dreaming. Never take seriously what ordinary people claim. For me, it is clear that only a bipolar brain has this capacity – not just anyone has this magic capacity and not all people with bipolar have this capacity. Very few can do this. When I was younger, I moved out of my body during sleep and when fully conscious as well. It was so easy to abandon my physical body! I thought, 'let's go' and I was flying above the houses and the towns, or I was moving inside my house as a ghost without a physical body, which I abandoned in bed. I went through walls and materials like a neutrino!

Later in life, I lost this rare ability because I started medication to treat my bipolar disorder. I am so happy that my new medication does not prevent lucid dreaming and now at the age of 60 I can conduct more and more complicated experiments on my bodiless awareness.[5]

What are these experiments, you might ask? Well, I experiment with conscious sex during my sleep. To secure

---

[5] I would love to discuss this subject further with any scientist who is interested. While I am fully clean from any depressive episodes during my waking status because citalopram works perfectly for me, a few times every month I suffer from heavy depressive episodes during my sleep. I have an explanation for why this happens, but I would like to discuss this strange phenomenon with any scientist interested to learn more.

what I experience as a conscious dream, I place my hand on a wall, door, or anything to check whether my hand can go through the object, violating the known forces of nature. If my hand goes through, then I know I am in the dream state.

Here, I may have sex with the women I encounter without being in the real world. Of course not with a human partner. These lucid dream sex partners are creations of my brain. They don't exist anywhere. They are not Earthlings, nor aliens. I am the creator of them.

The Benefits of Lucid Dreaming

The benefits of doing so are numerous. The most obvious is that there is no danger of contracting any sexually transmitted diseases. There is also no need to remember birthdays, flowers, anniversaries, and all of the things that occur in normal relationships. There is no need for human interaction at all.

For me, the biggest benefit is because I hate human body. I hate the misery, the dirtiness of the human body, and I hate to be involved in any kind of relationship with any sexual partner. I hate my animal nature every morning when I visit the bathroom for my bowel movement. How can I afford another animal to do the same every morning? I simply can't.

I hate to smell the gas of people in public places. We have to smell people's gas everywhere we go. On the bus, in shops, in the pharmacy, in lifts, in the workplace… everywhere. It has happened to all of us. How can I afford to have a sex partner to release smelly gas because she eats junk food? I'd prefer to commit suicide than to afford the smelly gas of my sex partner.

So the only logical solution for me is to discover this new sex activity during my sleep. It's astonishing to wait for the evening to come, to achieve such a miracle feat, to be fully conscious during sleep, and to have sex with unknown partners.

You are probably asking, 'hey Noah, why do you attempt this mysterious method rather than having real sex with professional women like you did in the past?' Remember from the previous history how I feel about this. It's simply not an option.

Anyway, dear reader, who told you it's good to have sex with physical partners? Who told you that living with a specific partner permanently is something good? Who said we must have children and families? Are we the same as all the other animals? Well, I am not. I was like you but now I am evolved and I can't afford to have the same attitude as animals.

Hey reader, either you are an animal or you are not. If you are an animal, but not a swan, penguin, albatross (or another monogamous animal), then it's impossible to have only one sexual partner. Understand that animals never do anything on purpose. They don't have logic to judge! We are talking about instincts and randomness. But if you are not an animal and wish to be neutral, try lucid dreaming yourself. Perhaps you may do something after a century or two. Be patient; we are not at the same level.

The Dream Game

You may also realise that the benefits are not limited to lucid sex experiences. Lucid dreaming forces me to conclude that we are all dream games and experiments of someone superior to us in consciousness and intelligence. We are all players in the dream arena of a Supreme Being. Many times in my life, I have wondered whether I really exist or simply play the role that a Supreme Being decided for me, for you, for everybody. It means that we don't hold conscious autonomy but are just bosons of consciousness, all part of *one*. We are not owners of ourselves. We belong to a superior brain and this superior brain is real, not part of the imagination!

This shocking apocalypse happened to me by writing this book. I am the creator of new cosmos and I am the creator of my new coming! Astonishing, superb. Now, think what the brain of a Supreme Being, the brain of the Grand Composer, can do! It's amazing because I discovered that I have the identity of the creator. And if I am a creator, then a stronger brain than me may decide and order the known world and supposed civilisation and conduct experiments against all of us!

Imagine that if my brain can create a living scenario for me, any scenario I decide and order, what can a brain stronger than mine do? I create worlds! Small worlds but worlds of another nature, another dimension, and another law! Listen, can I pre-arrange my next self in the next cosmic appearance of me? Can I set who I will be in the next coming life on any planet, not in the Animal Verse but in the Conscious Verse? Yes, of course I can!

At the same time, we think that we know everything, that we are the masters of the universe, that we have solved all of the boxes, and we are so proud of our species! Well, I am not proud of anything. I am just proud of myself and I continue to learn unstoppably. I have much more to learn and experience during my conscious dream life because I am only at the beginning of this magic world, and I will be here to discuss it with you in my next books.

History 8:

THE TWO SIDES OF RELIGION

I repeat my question from the previous histories: Who told you, dear reader, that being involved in a marriage and creating a family is a must? Who encouraged this social habit in you? The church, of course! Not any church of the current phase of civilisation but churches of the past. In this history, you will learn more about the two sides of religion, specifically my Mormon background.

The Mormon LDS Church

The notion of marriage and family was encouraged by old religions, such as Christianity and Judaism and Utah-ism. The Old Testament, the New Testament, the Word of Wisdom, the Book of Mormon, and various doctrines and covenants… the catalogue is endless. These are just a handful of the 'scriptures' I have studied that encourage the notions of marriage and family.

I happen to be a member of the LDS church, more commonly known as the Mormon Church, now called The Church of Jesus Christ of the Latter Days Saints. I am sorry for calling it the Mormon Church since our president, the wise Prophet Russel M. Nelson, advised all members to abandon the nickname 'Mormon' from October 2018, and more recently they advised members to abandon the name LDS as well. I haven't because the general population still use this nickname to describe us.

Anyhow, I joined the church as a mature adult and my baptism took place years after I abandoned the sexual holocaust. I was a free lion living in the jungle and I decided to invest years of my life living in the dogma of Utah-ism. Do you see similarities to my living with the victims in the sexual holocaust? If the answer is yes, then you are on my own spiritual frequency.

So, I joined the Utah-ism religion of Jesus Christ the American. According to Mormon scriptures, there was someone called Jesus Christ, who I call the American Jesus. He was not the claimed Son of God as other Christians call the unknown Jesus from Bethlehem. This Jesus appeared to the ancient Americans after he was resurrected from the Middle East.

I find this idea funny, like the American version of Jesus Christ, is the creation of Joseph's Smith fantasy, according to my models. This Jesus taught the ancient Americans who moved from Jerusalem to the USA by boat about 600 years before the birth of the other Jesus in Bethlehem. Hahahaha, what a joke! This is the true story of the American Jesus as it is written in the Book of Mormon, which is the cornerstone of Mormon teachings.

Of course, Mormons are convinced that they worship the same Jesus of Nazareth as all the other Christians. Make no mistake, it is only me who describes the Mormon Jesus as 'the American Jesus', knowing that leaders and members of the church may consider me an apostate for doing so.

Now, I am still a member but not an active one because I have totally rejected all of the scriptures, teachings, doctrines, and covenants of the church. I describe myself as a "distanced from the scriptures" member. Still, I am grateful to all of its members, missionaries, and leaders. I am grateful to my spiritual leader Russell M. Nelson. Here, I jump at the chance to send greetings to all of the beloved missionaries of my church. I continue to think of them and pray for their health and goodness. I still have a strong emotional connection with them, no matter whether some of them consider me an apostate or think I am cursed and to be thrown to the outer darkness.

Yet, at the same time, I would like to inform them that a lower form of intelligence can, under no circumstances, decide the fate of a higher form. Are they really so foolish to believe they can decide where I will go? I am above them. I look at them from the higher realms. And why am I a higher form of intelligence than them? Because they are stuck in their 'scriptures'.

However, this is also why my empathy for them continues. In some ways, I view them as slaves of their minds, but in other ways as slaves of the brainwashing they suffered from the very first moment of their birth by the church authorities. These are the two sides of religion: the individual's mind and brainwashing. I will give you one example of the latter.

The Law of Chastity

At the beginning of my career as member, I was shocked when I noticed that all of the young missionaries, elders, and sisters had so many brothers and sisters. So many big families! I quickly discovered that the institution of family is one of the main pillars of the Mormon Church, one that I fully reject. But why is family such an important constitution for the Utah authorities?

Have you heard of the Law of Chastity? It's a very strict law and doctrine, ordered by the founder of the church, Joseph Smith, and it prevents Mormon Church members from having sexual relationships before or outside of marriage. Officially, all young Mormon boys and girls must remain virgins until the first night of their marriage, so they have no option to enjoy sex other than to get married as soon as possible.

After the marriage, the couples are forced to start having children. Not one, not two, but six, seven, eight, or ten! Why? Because of the law of tithing, which I rate as the pair to the Law of Chastity, going hand in hand together. Each faithful member must give the church one tenth of their yearly income, or they will face the consequences. This is why the Utah government violently forces its members to only marry other members. They can't even *consider* marrying a 'gentile', which is what they call people who are not members of the church, though to be clear, I did see members married to non-members.

So, young members must create the new generations of members and ensure that the tithing business stays alive and profitable throughout those new generations. More children equal more tithing payers. In fact, the only thing that the leaders systematically check every month is who has paid tithing, and if they haven't paid, paid late, or paid less, they check why that has occurred.

Their marriage must also take place in a temple so the couple will be together for eternity, in the Celestial Kingdom, as the church doctrines say. Imagine that — eternity! This life and after this life. They ignore my objections when I say, "hey, this is not marriage; this is a curse! Leave me alone. I don't want to be with a specific woman forever, not even for five minutes. I couldn't afford such torture." But the Mormon authorities never have such concerns. The only thing they care about is tithing!

You see, the Utah authorities are aware that it's very difficult to proselytise new adult members, and on the rare occasions that they do achieve new baptisms, the adult baptised members often leave the church sooner rather than later. Even among their longstanding members, the church suffers massive losses. I have heard stories from all of the missionaries about their brothers and sisters who have left the church.

This is why the church forces members to trap their children into their nets from infancy. And the only way for Utah-ism trafficking to survive in the long term is to strengthen the institution of family and children within the current base of its members. It's not sustainable to expand the tithing business by proselytising new adult members. And so, this devilish doctrine of chastity was designed by the church authorities in Utah to enslave the minds of the young members, and it is one of the most horrible forms of people trafficking.

For me, it's clear that the church is a bank that always receives money from its members but never gives anything out. The church's fortune must be enormous. Nobody actually knows how big it is. The body of shareholders is invisible and unknown to even the church's members. Some people, such as ex-Mormons, estimate that the assets of the church amount to trillions of dollars.

During the era of my full Mormon commitments, I also noticed that all or almost all of our leaders who came from USA were working for the armed forces, especially the Air Force, or for intelligence agencies in very highly paid positions. I noticed the interactions between shareholders of the church, the Pentagon, and the Intelligence Services in the USA.

What do you think, dear reader, about this relation? Strange, isn't it? For me, it's not strange because I realised that the shareholders of the church have a huge influence on the governing bodies and main power structures of the USA. The invisible shareholders of the church are golden members of the American deep state, or the American oligarchical power, the lobby of billionaires who rule the USA no matter who is elected as president. (You will learn more about this in Part 2.)

My Profits as a Member

That is not to say that I gained nothing from my Mormon teachings, of course. This is the other side of religion. There is always more than one side, dimension, cosmos, or a package of physical laws, OK? The spiritual treasures I gained through the church were high class and very valuable and I am absolutely a better person compared to who I was before joining the church.

Becoming a church member was an essential, necessary, and crucial step in the journey of my life. When I balance my personal profits and my general view on scriptures, the balance falls heavily on the profits. This why I remain a member and will remain one as long they can afford me.

This is also why I still read the scriptures. Every day, I read the scriptures, among many other things, in search of information. But I also apply the Five Fundamental Principles in my private life, and I am on the Evolutionary Way (as detailed in *The Temple of Consciousness*). In this way, I converted my Mormon profits into a far bigger fortune than a regular religious member.

Here, I will share the three greatest trophies I gained as a member of the Mormon Church.

<u>Trophy One: Daily Reading</u>

In this church, the leaders continuously advise all members to read the cornerstone of dogma — the Book of Mormon — every day. Every morning and evening or any other time of day. Why? Because through this method, a member stays focused on that bullshit and day after day, their self-confidence increases as they read the 'word of God,' as they describe it.

So, I decided to apply this method of everyday reading to my own book. Haha, what a fantastic method indeed! No doubt, *The Temple of Consciousness* is the scripture to find the answers to many questions. But I warn you that *The Temple of Consciousness* is by no means a religion or a faith origin book. *The Temple of Consciousness* is my personal scriptures as revelations that I received from the Supreme Beings.

By reading a few histories from my own book every day, and I mean every day, I have gained the power of self-confidence and since I apply its method without a single day off, I am now in the position to reject all other books on this planet. You cannot imagine what that means unless you practice it yourself though, of course. You need to publish at least one book first.

This fact makes me a different and unique author. An author who reads his own books on a daily basis, learning new powerful pieces of knowledge by reading his own books. An author who dives into the abyss of his brain through his own books and receives revelations from the Supreme Beings and spontaneous forces. An author who rates his books as far more evolved and advanced than the author himself (this is partly due to the fact the large parts of the books are written under the guidance of the Supreme Beings who colonised the author's brain).

Finally, an author who no longer takes into consideration the opinions of people about my books, either specialists or readers. Their opinions, either positive or negative, and their ratings of my books are absolutely useless. As a result, I never waste a single second reading any opinion from anyone. So please rate my books for other readers but don't expect me to give a penny about what you think of my books, OK? This is a deal between the author and all the others out there in the cosmos of published books.

So, I am grateful to the leaders of the Mormon Church because they taught me one of the most precious brain properties, that is, to climb step by step up all the levels of self-confidence. Now I am a giant equipped with a demonical power of mind and demonical intelligence to reject the others forever without the slightest doubt or hesitation.

Trophy Two: The Gods

My idea of the Supreme Beings is based on Mormon teaching. This doctrine says that us members may all qualify one day to become Gods, providing that we follow the commandments with full devotion and faith. At the moment, while living on Earth, all members are saints.

In Mormon scriptures, the society of Gods is large, an astronomical number. This concept is valid vice versa — all Gods were once like us, living as ordinary people in the mortal realms. Based on that doctrine, I developed my model of the Supreme Beings and the society of the Composers as the highest form of intelligence, all of us at once, forever.

The Supreme Beings are the last step of evolvement before we advance into the society of the Composers, a society that is my own personal target to join. This target is my main motivation and life fuel to continue fighting like a lion against all the residents of the mortal realms.

Both the Supreme Beings and the Composers live outside the Animal Verse and it's up to them to reach us, not for us to reach them. We may only have the privilege as consciousness carriers to contact the Supreme Beings but not the Composers and invite them to colonise our brains. The Supreme Beings have the duty to watch and observe us from above, conducting experiments against us inferiors, among their other duties. (Please see *The Temple of Consciousness* for further details.)

For this reason, I call myself an 'evolved Mormon', something that by no means is acceptable to any member or leader of my church, but as I said, an evolved entity never takes into account the opinion of a less evolved one.

<u>Trophy Three: Family History</u>

In the Mormon Church, all saints are called upon to build a family history, giving our ancestors a chance after their death to be saved via a covenant that takes place in Mormon temples.

The family history search must be applied systematically and it requires a huge effort from all of its members. During this search, we go centuries back in time and sometimes even millennia. Personally, I succeeded in going two and a half centuries back into my family history. This search was exceptionally complicated because of the various foreign powers that took control of my island in various eras. But thanks to the British colonisation of the island, which took place between 1878–1959, I was lucky to discover some precious archives about the population of the island before, during, and after the British colonisation.

A family history is useful because you may understand some of your behaviours, spontaneous selections, and diseases that may run in your genetic tree. For example, since childhood, I have spontaneously felt friendly and familiar with the book of the Quran and the Muslim people. To my pleasant surprise, during my family search voyage, I confirmed that my mother's ancestors moved to Cyprus from the Ottoman lands in the early 19th century as immigrants because Cyprus was part of the Ottoman empire till 1878. What a background indeed!

In addition, as a Mormon, I am member of the House of Israel and I am an adopted member of the Efrem tribe. As from my father, I am not an Earthling. I prefer this term rather than the alien, because people may perceive crazy things about the word 'alien'. According to my observations, all of us Aspergerians, my father and myself included, are not from this world. So, it is unthinkable for me as an Aspergian to have any nation, homeland, or similar bullshit.

Now, aside from those heritages, I have built my own personality. I alone am an emerged form of intelligence, a strange form, a complicated form. I carry two genetic foundations, which are two black flamingos in the pool of my genes. Based on those two foundations and my unique self-taught method, I am here to present this unique book to you as a priesthood holder given to me from both the Supreme Beings and from Jesus Christ through the holders of the priesthood keys by His representatives on Earth, who are my church leaders.

The Priesthood Holder

During my active days as a member of the Mormon Church, we welcomed a lot of guests every Sunday, people from other countries who were visiting south Cyprus either as tourists or to work. Once, a cruise ship full of Americans arrived in Limassol, many of them faithful Mormon Church members and the chapel proved too small to accommodate the large number of visitors.

That Sunday morning, I was very pleased and enthusiastic. I met, among others, a wonderful lady from California who took pictures of us and I hope she still remembers me. I said that her eyes were the most beautiful, clever, and brightest blue eyes I've ever seen in my life. Yes, I became a little romantic and I could easily have created a nice, comfortable, and happy relationship with that lady, and at the same time ruined all of my principles about relationships.

However, she was a true-blue Mormon, so her only interest was in meeting the saints on our small island. She was just excited about the fact that our small island had such a big, international membership congregation, and I was the only Cypriot member and the only priesthood holder on the island. What a memory indeed!

Of course, the other members do not understand the two types of priesthood I hold. Once, I said to a member of my church that I have received the high priesthood from the Supreme Beings and the man started to think of me as an apostate. For all Christian churches, priesthood comes only through Jesus Christ. When I said that I have another kind of priesthood, he saw that I have a demonical priesthood.

However, I still hold my priesthood given to me by Jesus Christ through the priesthood's key holders of His representatives and I am not willing to betray my priesthood from Jesus at any cost. The priesthood is my gentle and humble pride and it is an honour and privilege to be selected from the billions of men on this planet to hold this priesthood.

So, please don't be misled by my own definitions of the unknown Messiah and the unknown Jesus Christ. For me, Jesus is unknown and was probably never born, and everything belongs to the creative fantasy of Matthew, the author of the first and most monumental gospel about the life of the unknown Jesus.

But look, we live together with people, together with these animals called humans and I am also one of them, although an evolved one, so I must live peacefully with them and compromise with some of their illusions. This is why I decided to keep the priesthood I received as I was chosen to receive this from Jesus Christ and still hold the higher priesthood from my church — and at the same time I choose to be a holder of the high priesthood given to me by the Supreme Beings. As such, I teach people about both sides of religion, not just the side taught to them by the authorities.

The Creation of God

Who is God? Where does he or she live? Who created him or her? Very often, I hear such queries from people. Well, here is my thesis: God is an application invented by the human mind. This is a natural thing to happen. As a species, we all look for a power superior to us, so there is nothing strange or unexpected in the phenomenon of creating Gods as supernatural forces above us. (As you will see in the next history, time is also an application of the human mind.)

The essence of God was created in the minds of our ancient ancestor human animals. God lives in our minds, not anywhere else, because we humans created God, not the other way around, like religions try to brainwash you! What an apocalypse indeed. We created God and before us, there was no God on our planet, but he or she perhaps lived in the minds of people elsewhere in the mortal realms, on planets where civilisations started much earlier than on Earth.

God is not a necessary application for our civilisation to run, unlike the application of time. God is not any physical law, which expects us to discover it upon our arrival. God's existence was never proved and it remains a matter of faith for us, without the slightest signal of God's power ever coming into force to affect us, with absolutely no evidence for the existence of such power.

Throughout the millennia and still to today, various religion-faiths have been created around the imaginary foundation of God by groups of humans who applied the higher power in their teachings. The building material of these religious creations was the fear that God will punish anyone who doesn't apply the word of God, or the scriptures, in their everyday life. The other building material was the reward or punishment in the meta-life area where we move to after the death of our physical body. In particular, the punishment works as tool to scare, control, and govern, the naïve and innocent people.

At the time, the masses of people were primitive in their understanding of the phenomena of nature and intelligent life (though many are still primitive up to this day), and they absorbed the 'messages' of the higher power as a messianic savour if they strictly followed the religion's rules. Through their mass of people, religions steadily transformed themselves into castles of economic and political power against its people-members.

Of course, any religious castle of power had the desire to expand its lands and follower-members. This is why religious authorities elected people in charge such as leaders, rich landowners, and self-called high priests and prophets, who forced members to create families and produce many children, as you saw earlier. They aimed to expand so much that the members would be equal to grains of sand. Indeed, family was and still remains fundamental in all main religions today.

Likewise, religions and churches still function as castles of economic and political power today, applying the imaginary higher God's force into the life of its members for control purposes. The messianic teachings of being saved from punishment are still pushed, under the power of scriptures that they call the 'word of God', a God who gave orders to the leaders then and now.

Truly, we humans are the creators of Gods, religions, rules, saviours, punishments, and rewards. Unfortunately, billions of people are trapped in such illusions for their lifetime, becoming victims of the seen and unseen leaders and owners of the churches. They also become wasters of their own time and don't evolve and therefore they fail to experience the possible profits of the other side of religion. I am sorry to them for that.

History 9:

THE APPLICATION OF TIME

The concept of time is something that the majority of human animals take for granted, constantly checking the dials on their wrists or the digits on their smartphones to watch their time ticking away. In this history, you will see an application of time in the flow of the present.

The Human Animal Concept of Time

If you have read *The Temple of Consciousness*, then you know all of time's properties and behaviours. You know that the concept of time was born in the mind of the first human who appeared on Earth, a primitive invention when man lived in forests and caves. You know that since then, ordinary, uneducated people have been victims of the anthropic nature of time, which continues to flow at their expense.

You know that this primitive concept was adopted by scientists who continue to argue over its properties. You understand that this is why human animals treat everything in their lives as individual events and why time slips through their fingers until their inevitable impending death. In this view of time, you live in the present, separate from the past and the future and therefore you are non-existent outside of each moment.

You will also know that I personally have never been able to accept the concept of time so easily. Simply put, I have never accepted the flow of time as an event in our daily lives and an event in the universe. Instead, I have viewed it as an application invented by the human mind to regulate the communication and behaviour of our species.

Indeed, I am not the only one who questions the concept of time. From ancient days onwards, various thinkers have thought more deeply and cautiously about the concept of time. One of those thinkers was Parmenides and I favour his views, but I expanded on them with my own applied model of unified time, which I explained in depth in *The Temple of Consciousness*. I will not repeat this in detail here but I will briefly remind you of the key points because this understanding of time is vital in how you live your brief human animal life.

First, you must understand that time is a human application to calculate our behaviour and to communicate with each other. Have you ever thought about this? We humans created the application of time simply to create order in our lives. Do you realise that time does not exist anywhere other than in the human animal mind? Or do you really believe that time exists and runs smoothly? If so, then please prove it to me!

Although the application of time is absolutely necessary for human civilisation to run, there is no need for nature to 'run' according to time. Nature runs anyway, with or without the application of human time. In my model of unified time, this issue is resolved.

With unification, the moment before your departure from this planet is linked to every preceding moment in your life as an integral whole. Every moment you live only makes sense if it is connected to all of the previous moments and all of the subsequent moments, to all of the past and all of the future. It is a wave function of moments, an intellectual manoeuvre that frees us from the shackles of time.

In this way, time gradually acquires a neutral direction and becomes unified. Here, you can stop hunting after events and create the events instead, gaining the great privilege of overcoming time. This new view of time frees you from the limitations faced by the ordinary, uneducated people of Earth and frees you from the agony of the moments that come and go. With unified time, even your human age becomes irrelevant.

The Flow of the Present

Very often, my mind focuses on what we call history. I wonder, who are all of these historical figures? Where are they now? Are they alive or dead? How we know if they are dead? Do we have any evidence about their death? Does anyone who died never live again?

Are 'souls' endless in number? Can everyone with sperm and a partner create a soul by delivering a new baby? Does a baby have a soul? Are all babies soul-carriers? And what is the scientific definition of the soul? The soul simply does not exist for the vast majority of scientists. According to my models, no baby carries any soul, nor any humans either, but all babies welcome in their brains the arrival of the conscious load, that is, all of them become bosons of consciousness.

During my process of aggressive meditation, I consider how the people of the past felt in their present, which for us is called the past. I place myself in all eras of known history. I walk the towns, I see the people, I create the buildings in my imagination, I create the clothes, I create the public houses for men to relax in, and my conclusion is that all people live in their present, without any worry or thought or concern that their present will someday be described by people non-existent in their present as 'the past'. They are all living in the flow of the present.

Do you have any concern that non-existent folks, unknown to us, shadows of the non-existent future (supposing we have a future, which I believe we don't) may describe your present as the past? Can the nothing, the unreal, the imagination describe you in any way as the past? Who are those people of the future? Do you know any of them? If yes, then please introduce to me one. I would love to meet folks who don't exist!

So, people everywhere, anywhere, and forever are only experiencing their present. The human animal separates time into phases: the present, the past, and the future. But think a little more deeply: where is the present? Which moment is your present? In the case of time running smoothly, there is no present at all. There is always the dualism of past and future but with no certain position, no clear position for both. This means it is uncertain when is the past and when is the future, since the present always disappears.

Do you realise, my friend, what I am suggesting? That there is either eternal present or no present at all. There can't be something intermediate. There can't be something in-between!

With my model, time is unified because there is only the present. We are all spectators and players in the scenery of the flow of the present. As players in the scenery of the present, we are all under the negative impact of the law of the entropy. We constantly lose. By living in the present, we are under the effect of losing. We even lose brain cells and energy while we remain in the scenery of the present, until the unavoidable time of leaving this planet arrives.

In this view, there is no future and no past. The future is merely the empty present, empty of events, while the past is the present but with events. Of course, the past is only our *memories* of events because something cannot be an event if it's already a memory. However, this is in itself a precious thing. Your brain has the monumental ability to transmit information from the present to the past, meaning from the one moment to other moments.

While we live and experience the eternal flow of the present, we have the unique capacity to create our past! We cannot create our future because the future is the present without events, but we can create our own past and decide who we will be in the past. Can you imagine that, my friend? Yes, decide who you will be in the past.

Your brain can transmit information between the current present and the past present. Of course, this process requires mental exercise. You can't do it overnight. Indeed, understanding and applying the concept of unified time is a constant exercise for the brain and a new way to engage with life.

The Theories of Physics

With this understanding of unified time, it's clear that scientific theories cannot be 'proven' because they will be overthrown in the future when new data and new observations emerge. This means that nothing can be taken as permanent because everything is a temporary thing until it is replaced by the next thing.

Imagine theories in physics. What do you think about them? Do you rate them as the intelligent work of some genius scientists? What if I tell you that all theories are not correct? They are not wrong but they are not correct either. Why? Because they are wrong for me as a Great and correct for the scientific community at the same time. They are wrong because they are based on people's observations, even if those people were well-equipped to make such observations.

It was not me or you who conducted the experiments or made the observations. It was famous people from the past present, 'famous' figures in the scientific community. But aside from being famous scientists, they were not separated from their origin as human animals. They were incomplete, primitive, non-evolved Shells and Shellies, just like us.

And of course, they are all wrong because they view time as an event. They take for granted that time is a fundamental event in the Animal Verse and always moves forward. So, all theories are correct for the regular scientific community but wrong for me as an irregular observer, a neutral observer from the outside, hoping that the higher physicists of the higher laws agree with me.

Going back in a reductionistic way, what is the background of any observation, any study, or any theoretical model? We often view technology, computer power, and education as the background foundations. But the most important foundation is the human brain and of course the brain power and brain capacities of each observer and scholar. Therefore, what we observe is what we can observe! It is what each one of us can observe and that is within our perceptive area, not an inch more. Our perceptive area is not one size, my friend. Me and you have different perceptive areas because we are equipped with different brain capacities.

This means there isn't any definite theory, only relative and temporary theories built in the very limited area of observations of the human animal. They are all temporary and disposable applications waiting for the next application to replace them. This is why I insist that we only observe one version of the universe, the Animal Verse, which is one among many others.

My strong confidence on this matter is based on simple arithmetic. The average life span of a human being is about or near 80 years. How can such an entity to be mentally equipped to judge events that have been happening for billions of years? Are you serious? Humans with such limited perceptive capacities?

Unfortunately, human animals and scientists especially create evidence that match their expendable theories! All of their observations are then based on what they have locked in their minds as non-evidenced truths and then they become the truth hunters of their own illusions. Yet imagine if one day soon, they realise that the big bang model is just a pile of crap and therefore all of the theories based on that model are invalid. Imagine their shock if they realise one day that there are no black holes in the universe. Imagine their faces. Imagine a day when scientists comprehend that the quantum world can't by any means match the physical world.

Here, I urge you to realise that true knowledge is the brain's capacity to reject what the others consider knowledge. To have the confidence to reject the others, their ideas, and their 'knowledge' and to start thinking differently against mainstream ideas. In this way, you can truly evolve.

The Fate of our Planet and the Present

As you have learned, we all live in and observe the scenery of the present, the flow of the present as I call it. The present means all of us, all forms of life, all of our activities and civilisations, everywhere, anywhere, everything that ever happened, is happening now, or will ever happen as an event on this planet. The present has its fate. And its fate is to die, carrying with it the death of all our histories, with the horrible result that nobody ever existed in this scenery.

Now, do you understand that the fate of our present is to be lost forever, together with our planet? That both us — the residents — and our house-planet share the same fate? And when we are lost, this automatically means we have never existed here. Do you realise that our house-planet's present fate and destiny is to be destroyed?

Did you know that the Earth has the definite fate to die? Sorry, you didn't know that the Earth is a mortal planet? Owwwooo, my innocent reader! Scientists are almost certain that as the sun runs out of hydrogen fuel (which may be some billion years away) and switches to burning helium, it will get much hotter and larger and turn into a 'red giant', eventually engulfing the Earth, which is the final end.

Would you like to live in such a present? To witness our planet's death? I don't wish you to experience such a thing, but there isn't any chance for our planet to escape it. There isn't any chance for any other planet in our material universe to escape from its present fate.

So, what about all of the histories we have created during our present you may wonder… Well, imagine the non-present situation when our planet dies. The death of our planet is the end of the present and the end of all of our histories. Who will be here to discuss our histories when our planet is just in ruins and dust? So, how important are our histories that we create every day? How important can a history be, or any historical event, or any historical human figure, when everything will be lost in an amorphous mass of rocks and dust?

Leave me alone. I don't give a penny for your personal history or any other human animal's history. My only concern is my own personal development and evolution and this is why I write books. My personal development and evolution are already separate from our planet's destiny and death. The planet will die but I will continue to evolve. Do you think I write books to gain money and fame? Hey, I don't need your money or your fame either. I only need to evolve.

There isn't any way to support, contribute, or change this world, which I feel such a foreigner and a stranger in. Isn't it funny that some people strongly believe they will change the world? How can they? Are they going to remove the wealth from its current owners? What a joke! I see many people who know nothing about what's happening on this planet but are convinced they will 'save' it from climate change, for example. Hey, wake up. You cannot save yourself from this misery and you cannot save or change the world. You are so stupid and innocent that I feel sympathy for you.

Twenty-five years ago, a wise and wealthy Englishman told me while drinking wine in a restaurant here in Limassol, "hey I can't change myself. How can I change the world? I want to stop drinking and I can't. How can I change the habits of seven billion other people?" He is probably dead now, but he was also right.

This is why I don't want to change or save the world and why I don't give a penny for the upcoming self-destruction of this species of human animal. I feel strongly that I am not like them, I have nothing in common with them, and I don't wish to be like them. However, as I said once, if one just person gets the chance to try to evolve, then that person has benefited from my writing and I am a success story. More than one is more success and more neutralisation for both parties: me and my dear reader.

Part 2

A COSMIC DISORDER CALLED EARTH

There is at least one rock planet within the Animal Verse that exists within the inhabitable zone. Here, we humans developed civilisation. Unfortunately, because of our animal nature as a species, we are capable of many dirty, ugly, and atrocious forms of behaviour, often in our doomed efforts to create optimal results. And unfortunately, the results are always in the interests of those in power, the giants of money, and the results always go against us, the citizens of the world and our public interests. So, unavoidably, we always fail because we are simply animals.

In part 2, you will witness some histories of our failure as a species, all part of the cosmic disorder called Earth. All of these theories fall under the view and observation of the super talented Aspergian Great Noah.

To help you to understand this content, I use Noah's theories, a package of models I created through decades of observing, studying, and meditating on natural phenomena, human behaviours, science, technology, politics, economics, and everything that is or happens. My method was and still is the self-taught down-to-upside method, while you always use the upside-to-down method, following teachers who are above you. I always starting my learning from down, alone without any teacher, and going up to reach and occupy the place of the teacher, therefore becoming the teacher and student at the same point. I am forever self-taught and forever a student of probabilities, therefore I strongly reject any decoration called diplomas, degrees, or PhDs.

At the age of 60, I am confident enough to consider the mainstream educational system as a useless decoration and I am strongly equipped to discredit it. However, I must inform you that my biological age is one thing and how my brain works is a totally other thing. My brain works as a typhoon and as a sponge, approximately the age of a 7-year-old boy in its astonishing ability to absorb new and powerful knowledge at the speed of light. So, let us observe the cosmic disorder that we call Earth.

History 10:

THE DARK POWER

The first thing you must understand about the cosmic disorder called Earth is that you live under the illusion of having power in your life. The reality is that you do not and in *The Temple of Consciousness*, you learned who those with power really are. In this history, you will understand more about their power.

The Dark Rooms of the Oligarchy

Ordinary people think that the regime in the free world, as they call our world, is a democracy. This is an illusion, of course. Democracy is just a decoration to cover the real existence of the power of the oligarchs. An oligarchy is a model-regime of power, in other words, a form of power structure where the power resides with a small group of people, who may be rich, famous, military, corporate, or religious figures, among others.

Please credit me to know accurately what the words 'oligarchs' and 'oligarchy' mean. Both are Greek words and my knowledge of the Greek language is at the highest level. Actually, the Western media are totally ignorant of what oligarchy means and use this terminology incorrectly. Oligarchy is the real regime of how the masses are governed worldwide. Democracy is just a decoration to blind the innocent and naïve people, preventing them from realising who the true rulers of themselves and their nation are.

Of course, the Western media only use the term oligarchs to mean the Russians with power, whereas I extend this term to cover the Western world's super rich as well. This includes the oligarchs in the USA, the super-rich families, of which there are less than 500 hundred according to the former Secretary of Foreign Affairs Collin Powell. These families control the pillars of power such as the Department of State, the Pentagon, the Intelligence Services, and the Federal Reserve. Some of these families and people are known to the public; others are not.

In *The Temple of Consciousness*, I described this oligarchical regime as the dark rooms. This is because the power of the oligarchs is unseen to you, even though the oligarchs are the real rulers of your nation, your family, and yourself. Politicians are just the marionettes of the oligarchs everywhere, in all countries. The dark rooms are the place where they reside, while the dark power is the power that emerges from these rooms. Dark rooms are a place; dark power is a force.

Cement this well in your mind: dark power is a force. This statement, this huge proposal is of great importance and it helps you profoundly realise how the global system of power works. The residents are people, but the power is a force. The force in composed by the capital — money — of those people, but the force acts as an emerged and autonomous force. Amazing, isn't it?

Most of the residents of the dark rooms are family dolphins. They are super wealthy families of capitalism who have been ruling for generations, or even for centuries. But no matter which family someone is born into, there are no special *genetic* privileges attached. They are genetically speaking people like you, but there is a significant difference: they were born into a super-rich family while you were born into an average family, or even into a super poor family living in a ghetto.

The Non-Governing Body

Once, I was asked if those in the dark rooms were an official governing body. My reply was, "of course not! There is not such a body!" Can you imagine these family dolphins sitting in a room to discuss the planet's issues and how to exercise power against nations and states?

No, they are not the official government of Biden (or Trump who was in charge when I was writing my first book) or any other who follows. In fact, I call the elite oligarchs the 'deep American state', as it goes against people's belief that Biden or any future Biden has any real power to decide on the crucial issues of the American national interest. On the contrary, those with the real power are hidden behind closed doors in the dark rooms.

Indeed, the 'deep state' is another way to describe the oligarchical regime of every state in the Western hemisphere. In every Western country, there is a deep state, which is the real ruler, no matter who is elected by the masses in the decorative democratic procedures. The masses are expendable humanity and the oligarchy of the dark rooms uses the masses and tricks them into believing they are free.

People might argue with me on this point, saying that they vote for their leaders in elections. Look, the dark power does not apply against you under normal and known methods. You don't vote to select who the ruler from the dark rooms will be, OK? There is no such vote. There is no such body of governors to be chosen from the dark rooms. If there was such a body, it would be a blessing for us citizens of the world.

Unfortunately, because of the power of money, the residents of the dark rooms have zero interest in ruling the world as governors. Instead, they rule the world as invisible dictators, while ironically some of them are very visible to the public but only for the purposes of media and publicity. Even if some of these figures are known to the public eye, their authority and power against you is informal, invisible, and untouchable; it is impossible to be formed, shaped, or voted on.

And this is why the residents of the dark rooms never sit anywhere to discuss things. In fact, they probably hate each other to their death beds and there is probably very little in common between them. So, there isn't any conference for the residents to meet together. They are not a team, not a governing body. They are nothing more than money and the wealthy owners of this planet. Just that.

You may see some of them having fun on social media, posting comments, or even watching sports! And while they watch sports like you, after watching that sport, they are still the super-wealthy residents of the dark rooms and you are still the fool who believes you live in a democracy.

Are you still proud of the democracy in your country?

The Smart Kids and the Owners

Here, I must also clarify that the residents of the dark rooms are not a group of geniuses concerned about the planet's issues and the people's worries, which some people believe they do. Though, in the lobby of billionaires, there are at least two members who have convinced me that they *do* have planetary vision and plans — Elon Musk and Bill Gates — but they are not the dark rooms' typical residents.

Both Musk and Gates are considered 'smart kids' by the huge oligarch families of the dollar. However, these smart kids by no means have any power to decide on big changes in the world. Why? Because they are newcomers to the world of wealth while these huge oligarch families have existed for decades or even centuries and yet most still remain unseen.

Let's say that the smart kids are the football stars and the oligarch families are the owners of the football clubs. The wealth of the unseen oligarchs is far bigger than the wealth of the smart kids. Despite this, the smart kids have massive influence over the people and could hugely contribute to an S.O.S plan. Unfortunately, they still lack a modelized S.O.S. signal and plan of action for the world.

Here, I remind you that at any moment, millions of poor people are struggling to secure a piece of bread for themselves and their families and millions are dying from poverty and starvation. So, Mr Elon is super rich because billions of others are super poor. Being super-rich means that somebody pays the cost. And that 'somebody' is billions of people. Always keep that in mind. If you don't have this terrible reality in your mind, or you don't care, then you are a monster. I am sorry to write that.

Personally, I abandoned useless 'luxuries' from my private life because I think of the people who are struggling to survive at any moment. Although sometimes I may look rich, I try to be humble, I help those they are near to me, and I donate to people unknown to me. Even if sometimes I go to places that offer luxury material things, I am very careful not to affect the struggling humanity. I seldom buy expensive clothes, I seldom go to expensive restaurants, not never but not often. You know something? Material things, luxury, and fame are all useless decorations to hide our misery and dirtiness, and I reject them because I keep in my mind the struggling humanity.

So, for the majority of the dark rooms' members, seen and unseen, my conclusion is that they are thoughtless people addicted to the power of money, that's all. This means they are doing nothing, absolutely nothing, for the global community. The crucial thing is that they are not geniuses by any rating. In fact, they are even worse than you in their horrible habits. The dark rooms' residents are the worst of the homo sapiens species. They are horrible people addicted to the power of money, which is equal to a drug addiction, to heroin, to cocaine, and to alcohol.

The Automatic Nature of Dark Power

You have to understand that their dark power is applied automatically against you because of money, because of the circumstances that were created during the decades of globalisation caused by capital. So, when you arrived as a new-born baby on Earth, you equally arrived as a newcomer in a prison. Everything was arranged for you, although you were and are totally blind to this.

Put simply, you cannot escape your family's and your nation's status. You arrived and were trapped in the nets of global power from the very first moment you were here. The war against you is unfair. They are the winners and you are the loser. You have no weapon to fight them. You are just a piece of slavery in the machine. The power of the dark rooms is applied against you. It does not consider you as an individual person with your own personality, but as a muppet. You are just another fool among the eight billion or so fools, which is the population of this planet.

Do you understand this? For those with the dark power, you are just a fool. Even if your family, school, social media friends, fans, followers, or haters teach you that you are something important, the hard and merciless truth is that you are nothing but a fool.

Truly, don't expect anything from them and don't consider them as human beings because they are monsters, devils, and forever enemies of us, the global citizens. They are our enemies for sure. Even if it seems like we cannot fight against them, the horizon of their wealth is no longer open or friendly to them. Their power cannot last forever; it cannot last for even a decade more than now. Soon, they will either be forced to change their attitude or all of us will go down in the self-destruction of our civilisation because of their greed.

History 11:

STRAIGHT-LINE VELOCITY

For some, there is the possibility to escape the destruction by evolving. However, the vast majority of people have stagnated and are stuck on a straight line, moving rapidly towards the end. In this history, you will see how humans operate under straight-line velocity.

The Stagnation of Our Species

In the past few decades, we have seen science and technology developing unstoppably and rapidly. I believe that they are now liberated from the gravity field and are both moving freely to new and astonishing areas. Of course, we can never ignore the fact that we live in the Animal Verse and so an outsider from the Conscious Verse would probably consider that we have only just got rid of our scientific and technological nappies.

Despite these scientific and technological advances, our species, the human animal, has remained stuck at the same level for centuries. In part one of this book, you saw how the Shells and Shellies have failed to evolve for a significant period of their history. This is because of straight-line velocity, which is my relative theory on the human animal's stagnation.

Simply put, straight-line velocity is the way that all neuro-regular humans work. For neuro-regulars, civilisation on Earth is running on a specific straight line. There is no curvature or deviation. It is a straight line only. Here, I must ask you not to compare a forwards/backwards move in evolutionary terms with the normal straight line of events in life. On this straight line, and because there is no curvature, there is no vision, no common ambition, no plan, no structural organisation for the total interest of the public against the interest of the individual.

This straight-line velocity of civilisation is happening as a whole because all of the species contributes to such velocity. All humans are involved in straight-line thinking, straight-line behaving, and straight-line acting. Ordinary people never feel any urge or need to change the line of events in their lives and create something different than a straight line, for example, to move forward, make a curve, or take a deep downwards step on the evolutionary line.

Let's consider a beautiful and current example of this.

The Spartacus of Tennis Example

As you may know, I am a tennis fan. At the same time, I am a master in tennis affairs, though not because of any formal studies. Please never bother me about your bullshit studies, or anyone else's because I am self-taught in all areas of my understanding of life, nature, and phenomena that affects me and this species. I am a master because of my eyes' capacities to see the unseen and my mind's capacity to go beyond neuro-regular people's perceptions.

Anyhow, I watch tennis competitions, including the US Open 2021 and the US Open 2022. The latter was special for a specific reason: a new star was born called Carlos Alcaraz. After a while, I noticed that everybody started calling him the new Superman. Actually, he reminds me more of the legendary hero of Roman times, Spartacus, who is better known to us as a film hero than a real hero! Anyway, I enjoy calling this big man Alcaraz 'the Spartacus of tennis'.

Of course, I must clarify that my Spartacus is not at the same level as the legends Federer, Nadal, or Djokovic. Alcaraz is not that brilliant yet… but he's only 19 years old now (as of writing this book). To compare him with these legends, we must go back and see how they performed at the age of 19. Well, I did watch them at that age and in my opinion, it's blasphemy to compare them to Alcaraz. He is certainly worse than they were at 19.[6] In fact, the next big thing in our lives is the young Danish Viking Holger Rune, who is a class above Alcaraz in his tennis ability and personality.

Despite this, Alcaraz offers me a good reason to enjoy watching tennis for the upcoming 15–20 years! Why? Here's a tip I offer you: when it comes to tennis, it's crucial to have a player to support. Otherwise, you may get bored of watching. You have your man or woman to support and then you also have a stronger motivation to watch other games where your 'idols' are not involved. It becomes a habit to watch and enjoy tennis because you have a reason to and that

---

[6] In fact, the next big thing in our lives is the young Danish Viking Holger Rune, who is a class above Alcaraz in his tennis ability and personality. Please don't be mad enough to place any bet on him though. This is just a prediction. There are no guarantees in this life, OK?

reason is your 'idol'. Everything orbits around that idol; otherwise, you have no motivation to watch anything at all.

Please don't think I contradict myself when I write about idols. As I explained in *The Temple of Consciousness*, I don't have any idols. As a world-class Aspergian, I am gifted to have a spherical view on phenomena, like a world-class tennis player is gifted with a spherical ball. But while you humans see from your eye to your nose, I see the world from outside to inside. I see the world from outside. I am standing on the top of the great Egyptian pyramid and when I need to, I can see outside this universe. I see you and all the others as my pets and my laboratory material.

So, if I don't believe in idols, what do I mean when I call Alcaraz the new Spartacus? Let's go deeper to reach the boundaries of straight-line velocity. Alcaraz is a paradigm, OK? I could use millions of other paradigm names. He is just my laboratory material here. No human has an exception to be rated as non-laboratory material.

Yet, I chose him to be my material here because I am a fan of him. A fan of a laboratory material, you may wonder? Yes, this is possible. For me, nothing is impossible because I know how to separate things, I know the order of things, and the order of my material. I know very well when I have to behave as a fan and when I have to behave as a Supreme Being against those who are ordinary people after all, without the slightest spiritual education, with zero experience of the gigantic and secret war against mainstream myths and illusions. Haha, kids and rats, all of them!

The question I ask of you to understand the paradigm is this: is there any chance for Alcaraz to suddenly stop playing tennis and make a fundamental change in his life? For example, is there any chance that we won't see him on the courts again because he decides to retire at the age of 19, realising he is not as good as the other beloved figures when they were 19?

Why do we all know the answer to this question? Why do we all know there is no such chance, that he will continue as all the others have done and are still doing? It's a silly question because the vast majority of people are moving along the straight line of this civilisation. They never dare to bypass this straight-line process and this is often because they don't know there are alternative lines other than a straight one. A tennis player will almost always continue being a tennis player.

There are sometimes exceptions, of course, and to my great and pleasant surprise, the tennis star Ashleigh Barty decided to retire at the age of 25. She made the choice to abandon the straight-line velocity, probably because she understood that this life has something more to it than hitting a ball with a racket. Haha, she is a modern intelligent hero!

The Global Table Example

I will offer another paradigm to you, perhaps a more interesting and known one. Is there any chance that Russia, China, and the USA will sit together at the same table to discuss the future of the planet, not as competitors but as *colleagues* or collaborators? Why do we all know the answer again? Because there is not such a thing, not such a probability.

Even you, reader, you are smiling now because you have already been brainwashed by the Western media propaganda that Russia and China are just alternative words for 'enemy', correct? You are already a brainwashed slave of the Western media propaganda that Russia and China are the bad guys, and the Western world is the good guy, correct? But can you place yourself in the opposite position? Can you think that the people on the opposite east hemisphere are thinking exactly the opposite to you?

Hey moron, people are just people everywhere, in every corner and on every inch of this planet. They actually have nothing to fight for, nothing to hate, nothing to separate, nothing to share other than the place where they live, which is planet Earth. Why do you have to support any of them against the other? It is because humans don't see things this way, so there is no chance ever to sit down genuinely at the same table with the Americans, Russians, Chinese, and NATO to talk about global peace and security. To talk about the prevalence of global interest against the interests of the oligarchy's regime.

And of course, this will never happen because the essence of the 'enemy' is one of the cornerstones of this civilisation, not just now in the current phase of our civilisation but always in the history of man, through the millennia. And if there is no evidence at all for an enemy existing, humans will create evidence to prove that the enemy exists. It's the same in science and in politics. Science and politics go in hand. Science creates evidence and politics create enemies. Even if there isn't an enemy out there, we can create one or two, three or more. It's so easy to create enemies!

Hey reader, is there any reason for innocent people anywhere in the world to consider you as their enemy? Don't be a fool. Nobody is your enemy; no one has any reason to fight against you. But it doesn't matter because the oligarchical regimes will always create enemies for you. It's essential to understand that for these regimes, enemies must exist. Why? Because if enemies exist, war exists, and if the war industry exists, then the super wealthy oligarchs benefit because they are the shareholders of the war industry, as they are the shareholders in almost all of the world's big companies. So, having an enemy is the key for any war to exist. (In the next history, we will look more into the Russia-Ukraine war to see this in action.)

Recently, in Limassol, I met a 21-year-old girl from Tanzania called Naomi. She is an asylum seeker and has an extraordinary beauty. Almost all of the young girls in Limassol from Africa are very easy to talk to and equipped with an excellent attitude. They don't smoke or don't drink alcohol either, which for me makes them the original female species.

Naomi speaks English fluently because in Tanzania the language of all secondary schools, both public and private, is English. I asked why she moved here and she replied that she cannot afford to live in Tanzania as there are very low salaries and a very high cost of living. There, a monthly salary is not enough to cover the rent on an apartment. I asked why this is the case and Naomi shocked me in her response. She said, "because my country is occupied." I asked why who, as it was the first time I've heard of Tanzania being an occupied country. She replied, "listen, epic Noah. My country is occupied by the rich… the rich people." Naomi's only enemy are the rich people of her country.

Now I address you, dear reader. Do you know who your real enemy is? The rich people of your own country are your only enemy. Why? Because they prevent you from living fairly, under reasonable conditions. They don't allow you to be an equal with them from your birth. They force you to remain a slave from the beginning, from your arrival, because you are not born into a wealthy family.

All of the doors are closed to you. You are blocked from sharing the wealth and prosperity because your fucking country is occupied by the rich families. And worse still, the rich families in power create fake enemies for you, you fucking idiot. You are so blind that you believe your enemies are in some countries thousands of miles away from your home.

Hey, your only enemy is living in your very own country. As Naomi wisely said, the occupiers of your country are the rich families in your nation. Nobody else. How much of a fool can you be to believe that people and leaders from other countries are your enemies! If you believe this, then just get lost, continue on your straight-line velocity.

You see, the human animal is engaged in straight-line velocity on the widest possible scale. We assume in our straight-line thinking that if we are a tennis star, we must continue to be a tennis star, that our enemies are genuinely our enemies, and that we must support our governments in invading other countries where our supposed enemies lie. We never look outside of this straight-line to see something different, a divergence, to do something different, to live in a different way. Only those who are neuro-irregular are able to see outside of this straight-line prison, to see a different way of living. Now, it's time for you to truly see what is occurring in our world.

History 12:

THE GRAND UNIFIED THEORY OF WAR IN EUROPE

Disclaimer: *Before I begin, note that what I write in this history and all histories refers to the power, to the political authorities of the various mentioned countries, to the centralised power of the European Union (EU) and the Eurozone, and to the tyranny of the bureaucracy of Brussels. I never have in mind the innocent citizens of European countries, who I consider as the main victims of this tyranny. I am typically one of them, of course, although personally I have very little relation with anything is happening on the continent. I am almost an outsider while living inside. I do have not deposits, nor assets, nor loans, nor finance, nor investments to or from any Eurosystem bank. I am happy and lucky to work with banks outside the Eurosystem. And I never love any bank, that's a guarantee.*

To truly understand the cosmic disorder called Earth, you must see past the veil of what those in power present to you. A hugely veiled area is that of war. In the previous history, you saw that there must always be an enemy because those in power benefit from war. In this and the next few histories, you will get my gift to you: Noah's grand unified theory of war in Europe.[7]

The Fixed Nature of War

Most people believe that WWII ended in 1945. I am here to tell you that the wars in Europe didn't finish in 1945 but continued in some form and have picked up the pace since 2002. Contrary to what most people believe, the current war in Ukraine is just a part of the wars in Europe and is not an isolated event. In fact, the war in Ukraine as an integral part of the wars in Europe.

To me, the Russia-Ukraine war looks like a fixed war between Russia and those in the dark rooms in the USA. Fixing wars where the nuclear giants are involved means giving information in advance from one side to the other. This means it was already on the agenda of the nuclear giants Russia, NATO, and the USA. Indeed, Russia secretly informed the USA and NATO about its intentions to invade Ukraine months before it did so.

This is why we often hear things like, "the secret intelligence services knew about the Russian invasion of Ukraine months before it happened." Yet the Human Animal fails to understand how this is. Understand this, the communication channels between Russia and the USA are always open one

---

[7] You are, of course, free to build your model based on your own observations and based on your own weapon of intelligence to understand and explain the situation. You may even present the model to probable others, as I do here myself. I am not inside the brain of anyone who is involved in this war either. So, I use my weapons from my own intelligence arsenal to build my own model.

way or another. The nuclear giants cannot be isolated from each other.

Hey moron, do you think that the nuclear giants are just playing video games like kids on the internet? They exchange crucial information all of the time. You may wonder why is there such a devil who would fix a war against the innocent people and innocent children of Ukraine? Hey moron, isn't it always the innocent people who are the main victims of all wars, either fixed or original? Actually, they sacrifice expendable humans for their own purposes, exactly as they are doing now by sacrificing the young generations from both Russia and Ukraine without the slightest hesitation.

However, please bear in mind that whether a war is fixed or not, nobody can decide the result. We are not talking about sports where a single referee or a few players may decide the result for their own fixed business. This is war. A lot of unexpected events may happen that nobody could predict or prevent.

For a thousand reasons or more, the developments in any war may surprise you. They may even surprise the fixer, whoever the fixer of that war is. In addition, the main game's protagonists could amend or adapt their strategies and targets based on new field or geopolitical information arising that day.

Here, I remind you that a target is one thing, but the final result is a total other thing, OK? As I explained, we cannot create the future but only the past. Nobody can predict the final result and nobody can *create* the final result because we can create our past but never our future. This dogma applies to this war in its highest and strongest version.

This is why I am not so foolish to back any of the involved parties, that is, countries. I am not so ignorant to support any political entity or country like a football fan. I never support football teams, as you probably know. And according to my model, those of you who you post comments against Russia and support the Western countries in this war are just innocent football fans, victims of those with power and force. You are just a member of expendable humanity, an innocent loser, forever blind. You know something? If you have this attitude, you will be the next fool to be sacrificed by the powers you currently support. This is why I strongly remain neutral.[8]

The Incitement of Hate

Of course, we are not encouraged to be neutral. On the contrary, we are incited by the media to hate our enemy. All of the Western media are currently involved in a race to see who can sell more hate against Russia. Can you imagine that? Why so much mania, so much tulip phenomenon, against a single country? And the people of this country? Listen, regardless of what the media tell us, or try to sell us, we must always separate governments from the people living

---

[8] The Lady Ursula, with her clothes under the colour of the Ukraine flag cannot apply her terrorism against me. I am neutral, Madam Ursula, and you are stupid if you believe that European citizens accept your psychotic behaviour. Your behaviour is totally rejected. You are just applying neo-terrorism against the innocent citizens of the EU. But who are you after all, Madam Ursula? You are just a muppet under the control of your owners, and your misery is that you don't even know who your owners are!

in a country, and we must separate government-puppets from the dark rooms controlling them behind the scenes.

Who decided on the war? It was not the Russian people, correct? So let me ask you something. Why did the authorities of the All England Club prevent the Russian and Belarusian tennis players from participating in Wimbledon 2022? Because of the invasion of Ukraine? And who invaded in Ukraine? The people of Russia and the… tennis players? The All England Club are short-minded villagers despite what they think about themselves.

I ask you another question: am I guilty and responsible for any rubbish decision taken by the government of south Cyprus because I happen to live there? Am I guilty for all of the corruption cases like Pandora and the Panama papers because the offshore President of south Cyprus is involved in them according to the international media and the European parliament?

Another question, where was the mania and tulip phenomenon in the hundreds of invasions of one country to another in the past few decades? Are you playing with my mind and questioning my intelligence? Do you remember who invaded Iraq in 2003? Who invaded Syria, Libya, and Afghanistan? Who destroyed the Balkans in the 1990s?

OK, I don't expect you to be equipped with such a strong memory and I know that you are programmed to believe what the Western media wants you to believe, but please reader, why don't you think deeper? Why aren't you suspicious about who is funding the mania-propaganda against a single country?

Consider why you are encouraged to hate people living in a country who have nothing to do with war and indeed suffer the deaths of their young men who are in the army. Mothers, wives, spouses, brothers, and sisters of armed men who are in the same agony and depression on both sides, correct? So, why do you choose to support one side like it's a football game and you're just a fan? Hey sheep, wake up.

I live in a city where tens of thousands of Russian citizens live and work permanently. So, everywhere I go, every single day, I meet Russian people and talk to many of them. You know something? 100% of them are against the war. Not even one person supports the war. They are all against the policies of their country. They don't give a shit about the Russian government.

Now they live here, they have nothing to do with what the Russian government is doing. I remember this myself from when I was living abroad. My only government was the government of the country I was living in and paying taxes in. The same status applies to anyone who lives outside the country they were born in.

Still, you might ask why are they against the war? Simply put, because they are people with logic. Who is so mad and sick in their mind to support any war? People are spontaneously against all kinds of wars. People without politicians and the barons of money behind of the politicians hate all versions of wars. They are the enemies of wars.

Think logically. Imagine Ukraine now… such a big country to suffer shortages in electricity, food, and water, especially during the winter. Can you imagine the tragedy of those innocent people? It's unthinkable, right? For all of us, it is unthinkable and totally unacceptable. But we don't have power to decide. The power is with the barons of money, the oligarchs, on both sides of the war.

Both the East and West are equally responsible for the human catastrophe that is happening there. This is why I urge you not to support either of the two. You are not inside the brain of the protagonists of this war, or any war. You don't know what is at stake in this dirty war, so you can't be an ignorant fool supporting one side while you are totally blind to what is really going on.

Don't be a loser. Just as they sacrifice the youth of both countries, they will sacrifice you without the slightest hesitation, my friend. They don't know you personally and they don't give a penny for you. For them, you don't make any difference dead or alive. The same applies for the massacre victims of the Ukrainian war. The barons of money don't know any of the victims personally. For them, anyone dead or alive doesn't make a difference. You are all expendable humanity after all...[9]

The Monetary Battle

Still, you might wonder: why is such a war being fixed? What motive do those devils have in sacrificing innocent people? Understand that almost all of the big wars in this current century and the previous century have a common reason as their background: monetary battles. The oligarchs everywhere and forever are seeking to expand or protect their

---

[9] When I say that for me, it doesn't matter whether you are dead or alive. Understand that I have a different background. I am not willing to sacrifice you! I don't have the power, nor the will, OK?

monetary sovereignty, no matter which ideological outline they use to mislead governments and voters. Everywhere and forever, this is the background of big wars like the current one in Ukraine, monetary battles using war-weapons.

Please consider this as your dogma when you watch the theatres of war, but especially the big wars where the main shareholders of the deposit currencies are involved. On the surface of this war, the USA is not directly involved, nor the UK, nor the EU, nor Japan. But all of them are involved in an informal monetary coalition against Russia and have China in the corner of their mind.

According to my models, Ukraine is the space selected by the oligarchs to transform their monetary battle into war-weapons using an actual battle. Unfortunately, Ukraine and the Ukrainian people have been sacrificed as land and people for the interests of the world's oligarchs who created this dirty war. The oligarchs will remain oligarchs in Russia, the USA, and China, while it is only the people will lose in this war. The people of Ukraine, the people of the EU, the people of the USA. Everywhere you find people. They will be the losers. You see, Ukraine is simply the first battleground in a far bigger battle, as you will soon see.

History 13:

THE MAIN AIMS OF THE WAR IN UKRAINE

In this history, we will study the main aims of the war in the Ukraine, all of them unavoidably and strongly connected with the main background of the European war.

Aim One: Flatten Europe

The first thing you need to understand is that the American oligarchy (better known as the deep state, which I explained earlier) decided to politically and economically swallow the EU. Why? Because they don't want a mountain between them and the Russia/China axon. You see, the future battle will be between the American Western oligarchy and the Chinese and Russian oligarchy. This is not a secret. Elon Musk, among others, rates China as the most dangerous threat to the American nation.

Instead, the USA would prefer a politically and economically flat area to replace the current EU. In fact, they would prefer a political planet-entity empty of power, just orbiting the American star. By contrast, Russia's stake in the war is to gain a political advantage over Europe by keeping Ukraine as a neutral state, although the USA and NATO will hardly accept this, so the war may continue for years. For me, the obvious profit for Russia, apart from its strategic national plans in the area, is the land in the south-west of Ukraine, which one of the richest lands in the world for precious minerals and natural resources worth of trillions of dollars.[10]

To achieve the USA's aims, everything in between the USA and Russia/China must be swallowed or become neutral or satellite zone. As a result, Europe is now becoming a full puppet of the USA. For this reason, Europe has been forced by the American oligarchy to apply sanctions against Russia. However, these sanctions will punish Europe herself and will punish the European citizens more than they will punish Russia! Indeed, all European citizens will suffer heavily from the sanctions applied against Russia and so Europe has shot herself in the foot. Yet nothing is crazy, nothing is madness here in the latter days of this species.

One major sanction is in the supply of gas. For decades, Russia has supplied cheap natural gas to Europe. Now, the supply has largely been cut and no one can guarantee that Russia will not cut the supply to 100% in the near future. Of course, the European politicians didn't secure alternative gas routes before deciding on this crucial sanction, which is ludicrous because energy is vital. The probable outcome of this sanction is a shortage in energy during winters of 2023 and 2024. A shortage in energy means, among other things, very expensive energy bills for citizens, heavy consequences in the German and in European industries, and social misery in European societies. (Some people are saying that Germany has already entered the deindustrialization era and the US economy will take advantage of that deindustrialization.)

So, the aim is for Russia to lose her throne as the number one provider of energy to Europe, while the USA's private

---

[10] Information from the Washington Post.

investors in shale gas will steadily replace Russia's cheap gas by providing Europe with expensive American Liquefied Natural Gas (LNG).[vi] Anybody with just a hint of logic can understand this. What does it actually mean to get rid of the dependency on Russia for natural gas and oil? Why is there this racism against Russia who have proven to be reliable and cheap provider of natural gas and oil for decades? Just to sell the shale gas of the USA's investors to the idiot Europeans in the LNG form at a much higher cost?

You see, this war is key for the fuel supply to change routes. The route will become USA to Europe, among other routes of course because Europe does not have the necessary infrastructure to receive huge amounts of the American LNG. The USA supplies LNG to many other countries so they can't be totally at the disposal of Europe in providing LNG, which is transferred by ships. LNG is a natural gas that has been cooled to $-260°$ F ($-162°$ C), changing it from a gas into a liquid that is 1/600th of its original volume. This dramatic reduction allows it to be shipped safely and efficiently aboard specially designed LNG vessels.

The difference between before and after the war is simple: before, the gas supply from Russia to Europe was through pipelines while afterwards, it's through pipelines and ships. In any case, I remind you that Russia has already signed multi-year contracts with China, India, and other states (including European ones) for the exportation of natural gas in its LNG form, and oil. It is also well-known that many European countries continue to buy Russian natural gas.

In any case, I am not willing to place myself as an author in the arena of natural gas battles. I would never risk placing the beauty and intelligence of my book in the energy debate battles between the EU countries. I will leave them alone.

Aim Two: Flood Europe

Another aim is to overflow or flood of Europe with a tsunami of immigrants from Africa and Asia, plus obviously millions of Ukrainian refugees. Indeed, one of the worst consequences of the war in Ukraine is the impoverishment of the already poor countries of the third world. The third world is now heavily suffering from a shortage of basic foods such as grain. The designers of this tsunami wave are the American oligarchs, who knew in advance that this would happen. With life being so tough in these countries, citizens have absolutely no reason to stay in their mother country. To do what there? To wait for their death from misery, starvation, depression, and unemployment?

The sad reality is that while large numbers of people are suffering a catastrophe in their personal lives and in their dreams to build a normal life, they become expendable humanity to those with power within just a day. And through this immigration flood, Europe will become destabilised until it becomes forever weak politically and economically.

What do you think, that the European citizens will benefit from this war? What a joke! I can only see an earthquake destabilising their lives. Hey, those of you who live in Europe, prepare to see a tsunami of immigrants knocking on your door. In *The Temple of Consciousness*, I discussed the topic of immigration in great depth. In my second book, I can no longer support uncontrolled immigration. I am intelligent enough to change my thesis when stronger evidence is presented and when a situation changes and now I am strongly against uncontrolled immigration.

Simply put, there is no space for more people. Those wishing to migrate must understand this and must take into account that Europe doesn't want them. Europe is a big trafficker of people to Africa and Asia. Of course, I mean the big European countries such as Germany and her satellites, who transfer their political decisions from national level to European level through the European commission, which is under the political control of Germany.

Through the commission, Germany forces the southern countries to accept all asylum seeker applications, knowing in advance that all those seekers want to move to Germany and the other north European countries, not stay in the southern region of the EU.

Listen, nobody wants to stay in the South, nobody gives a shit about the South. I meet many asylum seekers here in Limassol and I talk to them. I can tell you for sure that nobody from Africa has the goal to come to Cyprus. In fact, this country is totally unknown to them before their arrival here! Indeed, 100% of the asylum seekers in Cyprus want to move to Germany and other northern countries. Germany knows this very well and the politicians of Germany are aware of the fact that their citizen voters will become angry if they see a new wave of migration there, so Germany traffics them and forces them to stay here forever like residents of a concentration camp.

Meanwhile, they violently and unethically force the South to accept all of the poor people or face the consequences. They force the governments of the southern members — all of them totally corrupt, of course — to include funds in their spending budget to financially support the asylum seekers, or they will be excluded from access to all European funding programs. What tyranny indeed!

You might wonder why Germany and the other countries from the North force them to stay here and not go anywhere else, especially not return to their home countries? Well, this is the crucial point, my friend! Because if they return to their countries, they will spread the message to everyone, "hey, don't waste your time travelling to Europe as you'll only end up in Cyprus, Greece, Italy, or Spain, and you will be held there like prisoners in concentration camps. Find a way to go directly to Germany, France, Holland, or Sweden!" So, in the South they must stay.

What a shame, what a downgraded system, what a devil is politics in the EU! The devil is the governor and the master of the EU. Well, I hate the devilish politicians, I hate all dictators and all dictatorships, and the EU is the worst of them. It's my horrible nightmare and every day I think that everybody would be happier if the EU ceased to exist. It started as a union of solidarity and freedom, and now it has emerged as the worst form of dictatorship ever invented by the human mind. The EU is a fucking human trafficker and all immigrants must keep that fact in their minds.

Thankfully, the end of the EU looks nearer than never before and I expect to see the catastrophe starting this winter. The citizens of European countries are not so stupid are not such masochists to not be able to shower or pour water on their foreheads, to suffer the cold or even die from it just because their fucking politicians decided to shoot themselves in the feet.

So, let's observe the end of Europe together and let's celebrate for 40 days by popping champagne and dancing in the streets and squares. Hey Europe, just fuck off and go to hell. Though I am second here as Victoria Nuland, the diplomat from the USA, was the first to say "fuck Europe". However, if you think that after this war, you will live in peace and harmony, then I gift this world to you. Put simply, we can't meet each other here or anywhere.

Aim Three: Distraction

Hey, wake up! For dirty politicians — because the word politician means dirtiness — Putin is a blessing and their best colleague, distracting the public from what each dirty politician is doing! Indeed, a very common habit within the politician community is to use or create foreign affairs for the purpose of cheating the citizens and voters — with the 'support' of the media — to disorient and distract their citizens from the very serious internal affairs going on.

I guess you and everybody remembers the situation in the UK before the war in Ukraine, but in case you don't, the government and especially the prime minister were just a step away from resigning or being forced to resign due to various scandals and political failures.

This is why during the early days of the war in Ukraine, when the Western world was totally paranoid, I heard the Prime Minister clown Boris Johnson speaking Ukrainian! I laughed for several minutes. What a relief the war was for him. What a temporary distraction from his antics.

Unfortunately for him, the scandals and failures were mountainous and the pressure from the British citizens created a dynamic against the ministers and parliamentary members of the Conservative party, who were forced to resign one after the other until the clown Johnson couldn't afford to stay and resigned as well. Then a new clown arrived, Liz Truss, and everyone forgot about the scandals of before.

Truss followed the fate of Johnson and was forced to resign, and now the UK has another prime minister in charge, the super-rich Rishi Sunak! My beloved Joti, my housekeeper from India, celebrated when the news about Sunak was released! She said to me, "India rules the UK!"

Joti is very proud of Sunak because he is from India and he is a Hindu, the same as she is. I tried to wake her up and said to her, "hey, you are a housekeeper and he is a multi-millionaire, and he is a British citizen. You have nothing in common," but Joti doesn't care about these details. She is proud and happy. And because I respect my beloved Joti, I decided to support this new prime minister, just for her.

Aim Four: The US Dollar

Before 1971, the dollar was backed by gold. After 1971, it was backed by the blood of innocents.

During the gold standard system (the monetary system between the colonial powers), each country issued money according to the value of its gold holdings. I remind you that during the standard gold system, the world was shared mostly by colonial powers. There was no independent Africa, for example, no independent India nor many of the other countries we see today. So, the trading between the colonial powers worked smoothly with the gold standard because everybody was involved in the race to discover gold in the colonies, in addition to the existing gold holdings in the lands of the colonial powers. Countries rich in gold like the USA were strong monetary countries. To issue paper money, countries had to either produce gold or buy it.

The gold standard model would not work today for many reasons. It is impossible to return to such model because many countries would be automatically bankrupted due to a lack of quantities of the commodity. We live in a bigger world now, where we use more money, and the gold reserves in many countries could in no way back their currencies. Now, countries issue money from nothing, from thin air. Money is now backed by faith in the currency from buyers and international markets.

The US government followed the switch from the gold standard in 1971. Since then, the dollar has enjoyed being the de facto safest currency in the world because the USA is the most powerful country in the world. Yet, during and after the pandemic, the USA was a step away from falling into chaos as the dollar was in grave danger of losing to the other world currencies, according to my theories.

What caused this emergency economic situation in the USA? Well, it was a consequence of the pandemic and the anomaly in the food supply chain, which was caused by restrictions and lockdowns. As a result, faith in the dollar could fall from the international markets.

A necessary avoidance of this consequence urged the federal reserve to rescue the US economy by supplying the US market, i.e., banks, with fresh new money, totalling trillions of dollars. This meant a well-known multi-trillion renewal of the dollar, which is now in a quantity expansion renewal process.

However, for the dollar to remain a truly safe haven for investors and buyers, it must prove its strength from time to time by creating wars as the dollar is backed by the US military. The dollar means wars among other things. The dollar means military power and military power means a positive influence on international markets. Without the war in Ukraine, the dollar would have suffered heavy losses. The renewal quantity expansion from nothing is not without negative effects somewhere.

A war was the solution, a decompression tool for the dollar before coming to the surface of the international markets. Indeed, after months of war in Ukraine, everything works perfectly for the dollar again! Without the war, the USA economy would have suffered heavily from inflation, unemployment, and poverty among large parts of the American population, an extremely dangerous cocktail of factors that would cause massive social disorder and political anarchy.

My conclusion is that the USA massively profited from the war as a world monetary dominant, while Russia gained huge economic potential over the occupation of the north-east land of Ukraine, some of the richest lands in the world for mineral and natural resources. What a bloody business of fixing wars between the two nuclear giants indeed.

The next renewal of the dollar will happen soon, perhaps after a few years. Then a new war must be created to confirm the military power of USA as the backbone of the dollar. And again, the media will mislead you that the war was caused by a maniac psychopath leader who wants to destroy you and your nation. But now you know better and you can look below the surface.

So, anytime you see a paper dollar in your wallet or someone else's, think how this paper is backed by the blood of the innocents worldwide. We live in the devilish version of the reality, the Animal Verse and here, the currency that prevails is the US dollar, the devil's currency without a doubt.

Aim Five: The Holy Grail

The final aim of the war is the holy grail: the potential expansion of the human animal's life span of over 100 years old, though only for the super wealthy, of course.

The residents of the dark rooms are aware of the fact that the human life span can be extended to at least 100 years. Here, I am talking about the expansion of a young and healthy physical human body, not a decrepit one. Some of these residents even dream of being 100 years old and having the energy, shape, sex motivation, and appearance of a 25-year-old. They are striving to be the first ever members of humankind to experience the metamorphosis from old back to young. This is astonishing even to think about, so imagine how excited the dark rooms' residents are to be at the precipice. They are crazy to achieve this, to see it become the truth.

Strange as it sounds, this is not difficult for anyone to comprehend as it follows the developments in genetics. "Just give us ten years and we will make you look young, strong, and healthy, no matter what your age." This is what some scientists are informing their super wealthy customers. It's no secret that these treatments will be so expensive that only a few can afford to pay. Not you, dear reader. This is something for only at the most privileged of us, the super wealthy, the residents of the dark rooms. You have no chance, only to die earlier than them from toxic stress, from unemployment, or from all kinds of biological or economical pandemics.

Despite this, you are still the enemy to them. The residents of the dark rooms blame you for their probable unfortunate fate of not experiencing the fruits of youth in their old age. Why? Because you and all of us are 'contributing' negatively to their prosperity. Because of you and because of overpopulation of other people like you, there is a danger that they will lose the holy grail of all epochs. Overpopulation means overconsumption and therefore the climate and natural resources will be overburdened, as they are by no means infinite.

So, for the oligarchy to prevent the destruction of the planet because of overpopulation and the consequences of such overpopulation, the expendable humanity must be much lower in numbers. This is why I warn you to expect new wars all the time and all kinds of biological and economical pandemics. The oligarchy doesn't want you in such high numbers because you are danger to them.

Be aware of what is designed against you and your future, my innocent reader. The holy grail is not a negotiable trophy for the grand oligarchy members. If you are not member of them, then to them you don't deserve to live and you can't in any way be an obstacle to their biggest trophy of all time: the metamorphosis of their body from the old to the eternally young.

History 14:

THE THEORY OF THE EUROZONE

In the previous history, I told you that politics in the EU is a devil. In this history, I will explain my theory on the Eurozone, under a single common currency for those who have nothing in common.

Noah's Theory on the Euro

As you know, Europe is a union of independent states. Each state initially was supposed to have its own foreign policy, as there isn't any central European government. However, as time passed, the reality proved that no state-member has any original political power to apply a national foreign policy. And so, everything is under the eye and the interests of Germany and by expansion as explained earlier in this book, under the power and the authority of the dollar oligarchy of the USA!

In the pre-Euro era, the discussions about a common currency across Europe lasted for decades. Through these lengthy discussions, the final result was a common currency: the Euro, which was introduced in 2002. A common currency for those who have nothing in common. Personally, I laugh any time I discuss anything about the EU. How can you share a common currency with people unknown to you?

What is the common political background between the western and eastern country members of the EU? What is the common economical background between the southern and northern country members of the Euro currency? Are you kidding me? All of these countries have nothing in common, absolutely nothing in common, yet they share the same currency!

This is why Eurozone has all the characteristics to be described as a conspiracy. My logic forces me to exclude the naïve creation of a single common currency by dreamers and visionist politicians. Are politicians so stupid? Of course they are, without any doubt! But because of their stupidity, I would never involve them in any big, world-changing treaty like the Eurozone.

So, who created the Euro? Who created the Eurozone? Is it a conspiracy against the European people? If yes, who were the conspirators? Politicians or bankers? The bankers, of course! It was a crazy, sick, devil treaty that no politician could even pass through their mind. Some naïve people suggest the French politician Jacques Delors as the visionist and spiritual father of the Euro. I remind them that politicians are always the puppets and useful idiots of the barons of money.

Why then is it a conspiracy? At the time, the Eurozone was created by the rage of politicians — their ideology for supposed peace in Europe through a common currency, they argued. "Never again a war in Europe," they screamed. This rage and ideology of politicians acted as an excuse and those in the dark rooms snatched this excuse by the hair to implement their own plan.

This insane idea of the dark rooms was decided in the absence of the people, without investigating the possibility that the experiment might not succeed, and without investigating the possible devastating effects of the circulation of a common currency for those who have nothing common among them.

As we know, politicians cannot think or produce useful things or principles. They are only puppets in the service of the dark rooms' residents. So, for the naive politicians, the Euro was a pact of peace, while for the invisible oligarchs, it was the beginning of a war! Haha. We all know that the invisible can never lose! But why, and against who?

The Real Reason for the Euro

The answer to this question is: the American oligarchy against Germany, which may surprise you. The necessary intermediate party was the French central bank, which had connections with the American oligarchy and acted as the messenger between the Americans and the German Bundesbank. Of course, all central banks have obvious connections between each other. But why did this occur? Well, this practice was directly related to the two previous phases of the world war and is a continuation of the second phase of 1945. You should not isolate the creation of the Euro from the previous wars.

For the American oligarchy, Germany never ceased to be considered a deadly enemy. Although Germany was defeated in the second phase of the war in Europe, they recovered quickly because there were suitable circumstances. In the decades that followed, they were rising and emerging as a new global power, gaining global momentum and influence, as if they were the winner and not the loser of the two wars!

The scenario of horror dominated the minds of those in the dark rooms. The fear of seeing a mighty Germany again clouded their minds. "We need to find a way to stop them," they thought and discussed non-stop. And then, as a huge and unique opportunity, they discovered that the Europeans were looking for a common currency to build European principles and values on it!

This was a rare opportunity to act. And thus, the Euro was born. A way to trap and exterminate the German economic expansion was found. They killed two birds with one stone. They would trap and exterminate Germany, and at the same time, they would ravage the productive deposits of the European people with the Euro.

The explosion of this creation initially created a global euphoric climate, which some called Euro-euphoria. This allowed the states, especially those in the South, to have unrestricted access to lending at levels completely unthinkable for the quality and density of the productive bases of these countries.

As a result, the early Eurozone was extremely disparate. The fields of powers of the member countries differed fundamentally between themselves. From the beginning, there was the strong north and the weak south. After a seven-year period of Euro-euphoria, Armageddon began with judgments, but without limits. Instead of interplay among the fields of powers and the creation of a collective positive result for the whole spectrum of countries, conflicts among these fields spontaneously arose!

Of course, the logic was to unite independent states under one common currency, but today we observe that the strong fields of the North have neutralised the southern ones, as you will see in later histories.

The Structural Deficiencies of the Eurozone

Unfortunately, the Eurozone has many structural deficiencies and flaws, which do not show any kind of adjustment or correction. They are genetic defects that will cause the havoc, destruction, and the death of millions of citizens in the member-states.

Due to the strong need for the member-states' budgets to be almost balanced, there is tremendous pressure on the backs of the southern countries. Their governments impose fiscal discipline and as a result, the citizens experience over-taxation. Small enterprises in the South are over-taxed whilst being taxed by whatever is circulating in the area of economic activity. The consequences for small enterprises are unfortunate.

Millions of small enterprises in southern Europe and also gradually in the North, will have a mandatory padlock, which means unemployment, poverty, frustration, and social stagnation. The depressive phenomenon of padlocks is already present. Of course, the goal of fiscal discipline in a whole set of states with different productive structures is impossible.

Pacts of fiscal discipline and stability in a monetary union involving states with disparate productive potential will gradually transform the South into a region of forced labour for the benefit of the northern states. The South is already cramped beneath the fearsome and highly inhospitable environment of productive potential created by the Euro. Then the citizens of the South (workers, small enterprises, civil servants, private employees, and retirees) will be transformed into slaves to be sacrificed for Germany to have international competitiveness against the Asian threat.

The Asian giants are coming fast to challenge Germany and the rest of the European big economies. The Asian nations are progressing hugely with new technologies, have a cheaper available labour market, and have by far the bigger consumption base inside their own populations. This is a combination of deciding factors to violently invade the global market, leaving behind the current protagonists, especially Germany, whose economical future looks cloudy and scary.

Unfortunately, governments do not perceive the danger because, as I have explained, they are nothing more than puppets, gloomy figureheads of the dark rooms and the central banks, which are owned and run by the dark rooms. Meanwhile, governments do their utmost to be well-liked in the dark rooms even if they butcher their own people and constituents. Then they discover with horror that nothing changes for the better, only for the worse, regardless of who wins and loses in the elections.

The Puppet of Europe

Earlier, I predicted the end of the EU and the Eurozone, which I set at 2030 or even earlier. Indeed, when the Russia-Ukraine war began, it proved a theory of mine, and probably for some others, that the EU is politically speaking an empty box. But not only that… the war proved that the EU is a marionette of the USA, as I have been saying for decades now.

Understand this, everything that is happening in the EU is either an American decision and order made before the event, or it happens after American approval. I will even propose the theory that after the application of the Euro currency, the EU has been owned by the American oligarchy of the dollar. Yes, the Euro is owned by the dollar. You have never heard such a proposal before, correct? Well, it's never too late to learn new things.

Of course, I welcome you to please go and search for this yourself. Don't expect everything to come from my side. I have searched every day for decades to come to my conclusions. For example, you can start by checking who the shareholders are of the major banks of all of the Eurozone state members. You will find that the major European banks are now collectively called "the Eurosystem" and the Eurosystem, which is centralised under the European Central Bank (ECB), have as its shareholders some of the world biggest financial investment names. Then come back and tell me who is the owner of the Euro and in an expanded version, who rules the EU. OK, my friend?

The private shareholders of the major European banks not only benefit from the Euro currency as shareholders of the banks but also have zero exposure to the probable dangers or a total collapse of the Eurosystem. Among these shareholders are the superstars BlackRock, the world's biggest asset management company who have no less than $10 trillion dollars in assets. Can you imagine that?

I call them superstars because I like the way they work and of course I reject all ridiculous conspiracy theories against such superstars that they rule the world. As I explained in detail earlier, there is no governing body that rules the world. Superstars by no means rule the world. They rule the probabilities because of their influence, prestige, and charm, which they apply to the governments of the world. But they don't rule the world itself!

Moreover, they are not alone out there. There are many other super powerful people, all of them connected as vessels communicating with each other. Same people, different company names, you know how it is. However, BlackRock are the only ones who I have bestowed the title of superstars. Why are they superstars, you might ask? Well, the risks of shareholding in the ECB are tremendously high, titanically high in the trillions of dollars. However, the dangers are present only for the central banks who are shareholders of the ECB, especially by the exposure to the weak southern Eurozone states and banks, but there are no risks for BlackRock!

In the case of the total collapse of the Eurosystem, the superstars BlackRock would know the event in advance, of course, and could maybe even fix it. Why? Because they hire the most sophisticated and advanced human minds in the areas of banking, investing, and the global macro-economic view. It's not only Elon Musk who employs the greatest minds in engineering artificial intelligence.

With these great minds, the BlackRock superstars have applied scenarios to everything that is happening now in the world, or that will happen. So, don't worry about them; they will never lose — they will only win forever. They invest in all probable scenarios including the scenario of the end of civilization. How can somebody beat probabilities, you may wonder? It looks impossible, right? I too know that this is impossible. But imagine a company that invests in all of the probable scenarios, using all of the weapons, and all of the alternative ways of placing billions of money. Isn't it possible then? Most human animals can't even imagine what such people could do.

At the same time, think about who is investing through BlackRock. Who trusts BlackRock to invest and/or hedge their investments? Their human animal customers are the super-rich of the world. And what does that mean? Always have in mind that companies, institutions, banks, and funds are run by human animals. Not by robots or machines! This means that the super-rich they have super-influence over the governments of the world!

Of course through their influence, they control EU, the European commission of Madam Ursula, the ECB, and the Eurogroup. However, they don't give a penny for the Euro-parliament (or the Euro-asylum as I call it or a travelling circus according to Bloomberg)[vii] because the lunatics there are just useless puppets with zero power and zero responsibility to decide about anything. They are merely idiots shouting for nothing.

Although they are very highly paid to be the comedians of the EU, this is a necessary expense for the barons of money to show to you that 'democracy' works within the EU. But one day, the barons of money will sell all of their Euro-assets, leaving you to eat grass from the fields of Europe like a cow or a sheep, because you are nothing more than a farm animal to them.

History 15:

THE BATTLEFIELDS OF THE THIRD PHASE OF WAR

Now you understand the war better, it's time to delve into the specific battlefields at play in this third phase of the war.

Germany

Those lining up and facing each other are among the fields of production potential. The German powers look strong and just as in the first two phases, the first and the second world wars, Germany already achieved sweeping victories over the southern productive potential. On the southern front of the war, Germany has already levelled its rivals, causing an unprecedented drought of cash flow, with all the suffering for the southerners following thereafter.

There will be a sharp rise in unemployment, the closure of small enterprises, a scary increase in bank red lending, a decline in wages and pensions, the downgrading of the welfare state, and the serious downgrading of all self-evident state obligations to citizens, such as the provision of quality security, defence, health, and education services. Please have in mind that all of these predictions are happening at the moment.

However, I am not going to gossip to southerners or to anyone else. Corruption in the southern countries of the Eurozone is so widespread that it makes me question with what criteria can we judge them? Do you live under the illusion that the corrupt countries of the south, in addition to the inherent weaknesses in their production structures, can apply an agreement in budgetary discipline? What a laugh! I have studied all of the southern member states and I have drawn my own conclusions. None of them has the status of a country with international credibility and competitiveness to share the same currency with Germany and its satellites.

So, everything looks ideal for Germany in the early stages of phase three. But everything looked ideal for Germany in the early stages of the two previous phases of the war. The story repeats itself in a sadistic way, as if we have booked a date with history.

Greece

I will no longer deal with the case of Greece, as there has been tons of nonsense written around this subject. I will let them live their dreams, and the credit rating agencies, and the ECB, and the European Commission, and the thousands of analysts.

I simply stress that Greece has zero chance to remain a member of the Eurozone. It's just a matter of time and whether lenders will still lend against memoranda that never applies. It's just a matter of time before lenders decide to terminate their membership with special needs for Greece. It's a matter of time before the end of Greece as a member of the Eurozone.

It's much simpler than analysts think. For Greece, it's over. I foresee enormous social upheaval that will force authorities at both the local and European level to seek the solution of divorce. The cost of this divorce will be a few hundred billion Euros lost by European lenders, unless they start auctioning off islands and antiquities, taking advantage of the fact that the loans were given to Greece on the basis of English law.

By the way, did you know, dear reader, that all of the south Eurozone member states that received a huge bail-out from the European institutions like ESM, ECB, and other funds have transferred their sovereign powers by law to their international lenders? Yes, a lot of crazy things are happening in the Eurozone!

Nothing is ruled out, but Greece will be one of the great losers in this experiment for the common currency of those who have nothing in common. Nothing is ruled out as world-wide rearrangements of frontiers, exclusive economic zones, are expected — but also the fortification of northern Europe against the nightmare of mass immigration. Somewhere, immigrants need to be restricted. It seems that the islands of the eastern Aegean are potential candidates as places of detention for immigrants.

In the context of the crushing defeat of Greece in this third phase of the European war, the winner will be Turkey, who will most likely seek to succeed in managing the islands and managing the migration issue. In the second phase of the European war, Turkey lost and Greece won. Now in the third phase, the scenario will work inversely.

Southern Europe

As I said earlier, the first victims of fiscal discipline and over-taxation are small enterprises. When I say small enterprises, I always mean people, workers, entrepreneurs, and their families — in other words, everyone who invests their productive resources (whether as entrepreneurs or workers in businesses). I am talking about millions of family businesses and family members who fight like lions overnight, unaware of the unholy satanic enemy called the common currency working against them.

The tragedy of this case is that the people most affected in this scenario often support the Euro. They behave like the Euro is their best friend. Everything is to blame for their misery and failure but never the Euro! In fact, many people will be surprised when they read this book that the Euro is the devil. They may rub their eyes to see whether they are awake or asleep!

Of course, the propaganda of Brussels around 'the Great European deal' is so pervasive that the citizens of this place are trapped in a hell of delusion. A hell from which no one can escape, whether they realise it or not. You see, it's normal for citizens to be seduced by Euro-propaganda. After all, they have no defence, no weapons at their disposal to defend against it, especially given that they often have no time to study the subject themselves.

There is no free time for reflection. They are full captives in their business or work for seven days a week and if they have a little time to spend, they will be dedicated to watching sports or some other form of entertainment. The system of spiritual sedation works perfectly and they are all inadvertent fools. That is to say, they are not fools by birth, but their system of spiritual sedation has turned them into suckers who are working to enrich the dark rooms. This is how the inadvertent fools have come to regard the Euro as a blessing!

At times, I wonder about the number of applications that Stockholm Syndrome has. These involuntary fools, with no defence at all, fall in love with the very thing that has economically raped them and humiliated them without a trace of mercy — the Euro! They are proud of their great fortune that the Euro came into their lives. Yet their punishment will happen in simply a matter of time. There is no way they can withstand the inhumane environment of the disunified production potential called the Eurozone.

One day, they will feel trapped, robbed, and imprisoned in the worst nightmare they have ever experienced. They will feel betrayed and deceived, turned into physical and psychological rags. They will feel what girls from Eastern European countries felt in the terrible period of trafficking into Europe and elsewhere until the mid-2000s when the phenomenon began to wane. The overwhelming feeling of deceit, the theft of their virginity and youthful purity by lowlife bastards, will be felt by businessmen and workers in small enterprises in Europe.

When this colossal deception is finally revealed and exposed to the people, they will be overwhelmed with panic when they learn that the main cause of their financial catastrophe and their personal and social destitution, is the Euro, not any other reason cited by the treacherous technocrats and bureaucrats of Brussels and the rating agencies. The

Leviathans of the international system of misinformation who enjoy enormous salaries to systematically mislead the people. In essence, they beat you – the owner and the worker in a small business – and they are responsible for your failure and your economic destruction.

No matter what you do, these vulgar Leviathans will call you lazy and irresponsible. They will say you're unable to manage your finances, unable to adapt to new market conditions, unable to innovate. They will say that you are useless and that the economy has no need for you, so you have to put a padlock on your small and/or family business and let the big companies take care of the best benefits for the customers.

Here I remind you of the dogma of the neo-liberalism ideologies, that the consumer must always be benefited by the lowest possible prices. If small/medium size business and companies can't compete with the prices offered by the big boss companies, then there is no reason for the small/medium ones to exist at all.

This is what they will tell you and you will have no defence against them because you will have already lost everything. You will have lost your business and found yourself burdened with overwhelming debts to banks and third parties.

You fought with all of your might against an invisible enemy. You did your best, applying the best tactics at all levels of business, be it products, services, marketing, continuous staff training, constantly updating yourself on what is happening in the market, systematically monitoring consumer behaviour, understanding the conditions where this varies, and actively participating in all trade fairs related to your business.

You did everything perfectly with passion, dedication, and love for your job. You were always an exemplary professional and a family man or woman, but the invisible enemy was always there, lurking. The invisible enemy has a name. It's called the ECB, the authority responsible for the functioning and implementation of the Euro in your productive life. This enemy intervened, filtering your productive identity[11] to a degree of significant weakening.

You thought you were doing everything right, but that wasn't the case since the Euro came into your life. Whatever you do, the enemy is always stronger than you. Your productive identity, your productive DNA, necessarily entered a weakening filter called the Eurosystem. This filter, the Euro, is killing you slowly and painfully, like the Nazi gas chambers.

Before, your productive identity was freely marketed as a result of laissez faire and you were repaid for your genuine efforts in effort, labour, and drive in the context of your natural freedom. However, this went through the weakening filter to become an average productive identity of a total of factors completely unknown to you. The filter works as a blender, composing a mix of different productive identities. Before the Euro filter, you were an original and unique productive unit. Now, you are forced to mix with all the other

---

[11] A productive activity is each individual's skills and personality within their own national economical and legal environment.

eurozone members' productive identities, which are totally unknown to you, and in most of cases totally unmatched with your own productive attitude.

This weight that you carry on your back now is *not* your own productive identity, but a monster, a horrible and bloodthirsty monster that aims to swallow every drop of the blood of your productive identity. This horrible and bloodthirsty thing is the Euro currency and it will completely crush the South due to the irreversible weakening of the South's productive identity.

<u>Northern Europe</u>

Of course, compulsory and forced entry into the filter applies to Northerners as well. The benefits they bring, such as international competitiveness, are only temporary. The benefits of the North are brief because everybody will lose the war at the end and the bigger you are, the bigger the losses will be, and of course I mean Germany. Everything starts and ends in Germany.

Moreover, the filter has 'cared' for the North only to become a haven for millions of immigrants. As mentioned, the phenomenon of human trafficking to the countries of the northern Europe will continue at an unprecedented rate, and soon it will be out of context and beyond any organised control. Trafficking networks are always many steps ahead of the extremely slow and ineffective methods of prevention offered by European institutions and authorities. So, the masses of immigrants will be so huge in the next few years that the native populations of the North will become the minority.

The main consequence of the cataclysmic arrival of immigrants and their integration into the labour market will be to lower the living standards of the working-class citizens of the North, who will be forced to work for lower wages. Small enterprises in the North will find themselves in chaos and thousands will close on a daily basis.

Others will emerge as mushrooms that thrive in the countryside only when the Earth is watered by rainwater. Thousands of new small enterprises will have the rain of cheap labour hands but also the entrepreneurial ambition of many immigrants. The societal upheaval will be inevitable, the citizens will respond violently, and they will turn against the immigrants, as explained in detail in *The Temple of Consciousness*.

The filter will also completely crush the northern state of Germany, even with a barrage of fire on all fronts. Not only will this mean the collapse of the fabric of society and small enterprises, but German banks and large exporting businesses will also be vulnerable due the exposure they have in the south economies (BlackRock is an exception as I explained earlier). The central bank of Germany, as the bigger shareholder of the ECB, will suffer the heaviest losses in the total collapse of the Eurozone, and the central bank of Germany means the German economy and the German citizens too.

The German state will lose its international glamour and will be perceived by analysts as the cause of the disaster because analysts are 'wise' after the end of any world event. They know everything not in advance but only after the end.

However, this time there will be no regeneration through the ashes of the second phase of the war because the global financial circumstances are not the same as they were in 1945, where industry, technology, science, commerce, and innovative ideas based on new scientific discoveries had a bright field of application ahead of them.

Back then, they also urgently needed cheap labour hands and a large part of the UN Charter was concerned with human rights, immigrant rights, and minority rights because there was an immediate need to import labour. The ground also needed to be prepared for the smooth reception of tens of millions of immigrants into Germany and other western countries.

Moreover, in 1945, there was no such thing as today's Asian superpowers, which could sweep away the West, occupy vital trading industries, and replace Germany and many other western countries. Today, it's impossible to come back if you lose the war in Eurozone. If Germany loses the war, there is no chance to return as a world leader and giant like before the third phase of the war.

As a result, Germany will go through an economic glacier phase and its future is very negative. Either Germany disbands the Eurozone with its own will and intention, or it simply disintegrates as an inevitable development and will be crushed — perhaps more so than the southern countries. It is unlikely to come back to the surface of economic dominance for many, many decades — and that is providing civilisation will continue to exist on this planet, something that is also extremely doubtful.

No matter what Germany does, whether it succumbs to the blackmail of the South for debt reciprocity or denies it, which is logical, the Eurozone will disintegrate. The biggest loser will be Germany and the eternal losers, the masses, will suffer an unprecedented catastrophe.

The Final Score

I draw my own colossal conclusion. The conspirator-founders of the Euro, the American deep state of the oligarchy, had this goal from the start: the complete and definitive annihilation of Germany in retaliation for the catastrophe it caused to the global system of power during the second phase of the war, and as a retaliation against the mass extermination of millions of Jewish citizens in concentration camps in the Holocaust.

Of course, some members of the all-powerful authority of the dark rooms are of Jewish descent. Not all, but enough. The feeling of revenge is unreal. And he who feels so much anger, rage, and a thirst for revenge will do everything to achieve his goal, no matter how long it takes. He will conspire with everyone to succeed in his vengeance, which will bring him the feeling of complete satisfaction and superiority over those who viciously tortured and murdered millions of his people and possibly members of his personal family history.

The final score will be dark power 9–0 Germany.

Revenge is a dish best eaten cold. Revenge came 77–85 years late, considering that Germany's path to destruction will begin around 2023–2030 at the latest.

More generally in Europe, the filter that is the Eurosystem will cause millions of people to die of hunger, unemployment, marasmus, depression, and suicide. The Euro experiment will leave no one untouched. Post-Euro, Europe will look like a skull full of unemployment and immigrants. Nothing good is foretold and nothing will be the same. Nothing will be the same as before the pandemic and the war in Ukraine.

This will be the tragic end of the third phase of the world war, which began in 2002 with the official launch of the Euro.

Listen friend, it's not possible for a common currency to function smoothly for those who have nothing in common.

Listen friend, the Euro and the Eurosystem are the greatest and most disgusting plans of malignancy of the people of the dark rooms in order to humiliate you, overwhelm you, suck your productive veins like vicious vampires, and place you in the category of the 'global poor'.

Listen friend, Europe in the 21st century causes me disgust and abhorrence. I classify it as the most hated area in the world.

Listen friend, nothing causes me more rage than the Eurosystem because it is a deadly and destructive stumbling block.

Listen friend, in these last days, I am calling you to -defend yourself before your productive identity is crushed.

History 16:

THE TWO IDENTITIES IN THE EURO AREA

This short history exclusively concerns you and your productive identity, which has been castrated through the Euro.

Your Productive Identity

The Euro-catastrophe will start in Europe but leave behind ruined and dilapidated people across the world. I emphasise the word *people*. They are the ones who will pay the price, as always happens in every catastrophe. The masses of people mean you, your family, employees in the private and public sectors, retirees, the younger generation, the unemployed, and small and medium-sized businesses. In other words, the backbone of society. It means the workers and the owners of small and medium-sized enterprises.

You, the Euro-poor, medium-sized entrepreneur, the worker, the retiree, the unemployed, the young scientist, or the young man who is looking to enter the job market, have had your productive identity castrated so you are productively disabled for life.

You must understand that the Euro has imposed two productive identities on countries and individuals:

- The **general** identity that is traded in markets like the ruthless global Euro, which citizens boast about and take pride in because it's strong in the markets.

- The **professional** productive identity in your own country, in your own region, in your own field of work, which you must strain daily to keep at a tolerable level of productive performance, and it is weak.

In the latter, a laboratory mutation has taken place so that it is inherently weak. The laboratory in which the mutation of your identity took place is the ECB. The results of this weakening are reflected in the whole of your life: your income, which is constantly shrinking, and your subsequent quality of life, which is eroded by the stress of constant struggles for survival in prejudiced circumstances.

Your two identities function and are carried out in two parallel universes. The strong version is in the universe of markets, from which you have no personal benefit, and the weak version is in the universe of daily struggle in a working-productive life and because it is the weak version, you experience constant losses at all levels.

Your income and claims are constantly weakened because they revolve around the weak version, while your debts are constantly strengthened because debts revolve around the strong version. The parallel universes did not communicate with each other, nor did they meet until 2009, when the first cosmogenic change took place, which bears the name Greece.

In the case of Germany and the northern countries, in the first 7–13 years of the implementation of the Euro, the productive identities were reversed. The general identity of the markets were weak. The professional identity of production within Germany and the rest of the North was strong. This is why we saw successive big bangs of euphoria, growth, and triumphs in the northern Eurozone.

Then in 2009, the problem of Greece was announced, followed by other states. Since 2015, there has been an uncontrolled entry of millions of migrants into northern Europe. Then there was the lockdown caused by the pandemic in spring 2020. Then in 2022, there was the war in Ukraine. As a result, Germany and the countries of the strong general identity and the weak professional identity will face the inevitable consequence of finding themselves on the knife's edge.

As a result of the steady decline in your income, if you are a paid worker or a retiree, you will find that your monthly salary will decrease. When you had your own national currency and a single productive identity, a salary and a pension was enough for 30 days. You had savings to go on holiday, eat at a restaurant occasionally, save money, and buy a new car because you were credible to the banks and they gave you loans even if you didn't ask for them. You bought all the necessary items for your children and maybe you had the opportunity to send them to a private school. You had good hospital services, you felt more secure, and generally your life was smoother and less stressful than it is now as a Euro-poor person.

You had a smooth productive life. You had opportunities, visions, expectations, hopes, and enthusiasm to start a new business or expand an existing one. There were favourable and charitable conditions to cultivate your talents, your skills, your knowledge, and your experiences on an individual and family level. Together with your fellow citizens, you shaped the national character of the production of your country. You collectively shaped the character, the gifts, and the advantages of your country. You were collectively racing in the global arena of competition.

You were a member of the national productive race. You raced relentlessly and insistently using the arrows of your quiver and your country had a collective well-earned representation in the global competition. You were constantly carrying the form, the physical and mental state, the manners, the customs, the culture, the language, the religion, and the civilisation of your country. You had your productive DNA — as it was located and read by exports, trade, services, products, energy resources, geostrategic value, infrastructure, development projects, and innovation, plus the offers of the farmer, the fisherman, the stockbreeder, the builder, the worker, the craftsman, the scientist, the teacher, and the artist — all collectively imprinted on the national currency.

The national currency was of you, yourself, and all of your own country. Now everything is lost.

The reason is that the cost of living, including total taxes, was compatible with your currency before the creation of the Euro. Now, in the uniform of the Euro-poor, you are not much different from a slave, not much different from someone who is forced to work in exchange for a bit of mouldy bread.

The Internal Devaluation

A while later, your salary was enough for 20 days a month. You and your family were helpless for 10 whole days. You were unhappy and miserable waiting for the end of the month for the next salary to come… then you realised that salary was enough for only 15 days… then only for 10… then you adjusted and started counting the last cent, cutting costs from everywhere. You transformed into the toughest prison guard of your own prison.

This process of watching your salary all the time becomes shorter and shorter, as an internal devaluation. Of course, the weak member states of the South can't devalue their currency because they don't have a currency. So, the internal devaluation is applied unavoidably and this kind of devaluation doesn't require any official action by the ECB. It is applied spontaneously because there isn't any other way.

When the authorities are bombarding you with taxes, new taxes, VAT, and taxes on taxes, what does this mean? That your available income for living is violently adjusted to your original productive identity while you live and produce in the same monetary area as Germany, Holland, and the other strong productive forces of the North. Oh, my poor southerners!

This internal devaluation is, of course, informal. This means that its target is not to reinforce the international competitiveness of the South. We won't see a violent cutting of costs and salaries. The devaluation is applied only to the snaky method of reducing your income by adding more taxes to the most crucial products and services like electricity, water, and fuel.

In the South, your salary must be enough for 10–12 days of living because this is what you deserve to live on according to your productive identity placed next to the German or Dutch productive identity. Because you are in the same productivity area with Germany, you will suffer from starvation and have to shut your mouth.

Now you realise you are confused... but because you don't have the time and money to think about who is responsible for this distribution of yours, you assign the responsibility anywhere other than your real enemy, which is your currency. It never even crossed your mind before this book, right?

You're like a burned-out slave and prisoner at the merciless interests of big capital that has no borders or currency. Yet you think you're like those in the dark rooms. You think you're one with those who have imposed a common currency on you. And so you celebrate the good of having a common currency with the tenants of the dark rooms!

I saw this in the 21st century. I saw the happy slave! The slave who celebrates the chains that his dynasty has passed on to his entire productive body.

The logical conclusion of this analysis, the logical trophy you win, is that big capital is a phase of delusion for further expansion at the detriment of your productive reserves. This process was imposed on you by the Euro with the element of conspiracy to avenge the tenants of the dark rooms against Germany.

The only way to defend against the Eurozone is to take self-defence measures so that when the crash occurs, your losses will be as small and manageable as possible. Obviously, stay away from loans from any bank in the Eurosystem and of course withdraw your deposits.

This is my own practice. I keep accounts with them but I do not guarantee their viability. I do not guarantee even a cent. I have the smallest possible relationship with the Eurosystem, believing that in this way my personal losses will be manageable in the coming crash, even if the economies of the large and powerful members of the Euro collapse completely.

Noah's Euro Summary

As you have seen, Europe is cursed to suffer all kinds of wars. Can you imagine that? Perhaps the location of the continent or the old continent as it is known, was chosen by the barons of money — the owners of us and our productive resources — to be the theatre of major wars. From the first world war to the second and now the third world phase according to my models.

The current third phase started in 2002 as you learned, through the application of the Euro and was made worse because of the pandemic. The final shock was the war in Ukraine, with terrible consequences for the daily routine of anybody who lives on the continent. The European continent is now experiencing a huge survival challenge.

According to my models and by any logical viewing, the Eurozone is proving to be an unviable monetary zone. I predict that either the owners of the Euro will decide to shut down the Euro-experiment, causing ultimate chaos in both the markets and the real economies and lives of the Europeans citizens — or the Euro-area will steadily become a new Soviet Union-style federation. In the worse version of the latter option, the citizens (especially but not exclusively the average citizens of the South) will be forced to live on an income of €200–€300 with living costs of €4000–€5000. In this scary but not unimaginable scenario, the Eurozone may continue to survive as a ghost monetary area for a few decades more.

I give both results a 50/50 chance.

Friend, always keep in mind that the Euro is a sinister currency without any possibility of survival, regardless of what is said by those who are paid to talk about its strength. Always keep in mind that not one but *three* European countries chose not to join the Euro: the UK, Sweden, and Denmark.

The UK is now out of the EU, as you know. The two northern Scandinavian countries believe that any monetary union without a political union as a background is doomed to fail. They carry the collective bad experience of the Scandinavian Monetary Union, which endured for several decades, longer than the Euro as of today. However, it was disintegrated due to a lack of common political power (that is, a lack of a single state power), as is currently the case in the Eurozone. Also, two other European countries, Switzerland, and Norway, are not even members of the EU as this possibility was rejected by the respective people through referendums.

As you may conclude, the non-Eurozone European states may be the sole escapees of the upcoming colossal disaster. The UK, Sweden, Denmark, Norway, and Switzerland will be the sole survivors to emerge from the ashes of the wars. Not without severe wounds, but survivors nonetheless. Iceland will survive the war, because this small, lovely country has nothing to do with Euro and Europe. On the contrary, Finland as a member of the Eurozone will suffer severe wounds because its economy has had heavy exposure to the southern countries of the Euro. So, the future of Finland is uncertain.

The Eastern European states will continue to struggle but with better potential than western members. Poland, if she survives the Ukraine war, may emerge as a small version of Germany.

Either way, Europe as a concept is doomed to fail and will be the central location for upcoming wars. It is nearing its end, as is Europe and our pitiful species, the human animal.

Conclusion:

BENEDICTION

As you know, Noah's flood is a myth included in Genesis, the first book of the Old Testament. Here, you will understand Noah's flood of our own times.

Noah's Theory of the Latter Days

Indeed, I feel that the flood is already in progress. I am not talking about a flood of water but the flood of humans. I live this first-hand. I experience the modern flood every day. As I have alluded to, thousands of people are moving from Africa and Asia to my small island because there is no chance for them in their poor, politically corrupt, and unstable homelands.

But unlike Noah's flood story of old, who am I to save them? They have zero chance to be saved because there are too many people. As you have seen, the war in Ukraine has led even more people to seek asylum in their desperate hope to secure their future, as well as the millions already seeking asylum from their inhospitable countries.

They have zero chance because they keep arriving unstoppably. People are moving like crazy from one area to another for various reasons. Wars, food shortages, water shortages, unemployment, terrorism, crime rates, peanut salaries. Not only here but everywhere in Europe and

America, where they are unfortunately unwanted by the people there and treated as unwelcome outsiders.

They have zero chance because those with power view them as expendable humanity to use for their own purposes. You see, there is always the possibility that the dark rooms members will use immigrants to replace the local population of European countries because they offer a cheaper labour market.

In this way, they will replace you with an immigrant because immigrants are willing to work for far less than you will work for. And the less someone is willing to work for, the better it is for the economy to gain or expand its international competitiveness. So, either the local native labour market accepts work at much lower salaries or immigrants will replace them.

Who do you think you are, my friend? Do you think you are better than the immigrants arriving in your country? If so, what an illusion you live in. You are just an expendable unit like they are, nothing more. So, don't be a fool to trust the authorities and of course I mean the dark power authorities actually ruling the world, not their puppet politicians who appear to be in charge. Don't be such a fool to identify the interests of the dark rooms with your own personal interests. Do you really think they care whether you can pay your gas and electric bill?

I urge you to imagine the very near future. Imagine the world in 3–5 years' time. How many people can we afford to accommodate in our places? Who will work and who will be replaced in the process of the population exchange? Who will be in the category of the exchanged? You, of course! Bingo!

But this scenario of replacing people with people is definitely not going to work because of the flood, because of the numbers. The flood is a flood and there isn't any way to prevent the overflow of the dam of the social web, unless somehow the dark rooms decide to kill billions of people.

Add in the arrival of 'artificial intelligence' as a game changer in the area of labour and tell me whether we are nearing the final flood or not. When humans are replaced by machines who can do their work faster and complain less, there is no doubt that we are nearing the end. That is why I continuously prepare myself for the final days.

I am satisfied because I have gained enough power, knowledge, and trophies here that I have already prepared for my next coming in the Conscious Verse. This means that for me, the end is welcome! Truly, I will miss nothing from this horrible hell, from this devilish version of reality where I have been forced to live for so long.

There is a logical question you may be asking right now: is there any way to escape the flood, especially for the younger generations who haven't had time to gain the power or knowledge? Look, I'm not the saviour of anyone, but where there is a will, there is a way. Unfortunately, the dark rooms must have the willingness, not you or I. We cannot stop the flood and I am sorry for that. Ciao, my friend.[12]

---

[12] People everywhere are reading events on a straight-line velocity. They don't use the brain quality of collective observation. In that case, what do I expect or desire from writing this book? I answered this query to my editor: I write for my own profit. Not for money, fame, or profit. Money from whom? And fame from whom? From the animals living in the Animal Verse? To receive money and fame from a lesser species? The

The End of the Animal Verse

We live in the worst version of reality, which is the Animal Verse. The evidence is obvious even to you if you open your eyes. We are just animals. Animals that have been chosen by others, by stronger brains compared to ours, by the Grand Composers as I call them, to be loaded and carry consciousness. We are conscious animals against all the other species on this planet who remain unconscious or have minimal amounts of conscious load.

This is the devilish version of reality. I use the word devil because this word carries quantities of bad, ugly, wild, scary. Well, this is the world we produce. This is the civilisation we have built, which we feel proud of, and this is the reality we experience because our nature is the animal of Earth.

The Animal Verse we live in and observe is just one among other versions of reality. Imagine us, the worst and most scary scenario of realities, to claim that we know everything, that we can solve everything. It's pretty funny, isn't it?

We are cursed to live here as slaves, to consider ourselves the ultimate form of intelligence and self-awareness. And yes, we are slaves. The vast majority of the residents of this planet are cursed to be born and die as slaves. They don't have even a very small share of the wealth. To be born as shareholders of wealth, you must be born into a wealthy family. Otherwise forget it. The chances of going it alone to gather wealth are diminishing. There are always some chances, but very few can achieve it.

---

higher never cares what the lower is doing. That is why I write for myself.

Animal and slave. This is your original identity. The fact that you live within a labyrinth of illusions yet fail to realise they are illusions makes you as funny species. You live in your version of reality, which is the animal reality, a version of reality within the vast and unknown areas of dark reality.

Based on your identity, you are laboratory material for me. I use you to create experiments. As I am myself laboratory material for supreme forms of intelligence, you to me are the same as I am a higher and more powerful form of intelligence than you.

This is the line up of the intelligence phases:

1. Animals and known matter.

2. Animals with consciousness and hand capabilities building civilisations in the scenery of known matter and known natural laws. Here, the Animal Verse is an essential tool to understand where you live and where you exist, which is the second phase.

3. The identity of the creator, the brain capacity to create new worlds for who are not following the known natural forces and are running in other versions of reality by other laws.

4. The Supreme Beings, those with bodiless self-awareness with the power to create any kind of body shape by giving the order to intelligent particles. The Supreme Beings are entities who were living in the Animal Verse but have now evolved and advanced to live in the Conscious Verse, conducting experiments against beings like Earthlings.

> 5. The Grand Composers, the creators of all cosmos, all of us at once and forever.

As you can see, I have upgraded you from level 1 in *The Temple of Consciousness* to level 2 in *The Animal Verse.* Congratulations.

We are living on the wrong side of the veil. Never forget our nature: we are animals. We kill to survive and the strongest within the species are the most animalistic in their habits and behaviours.

Remember that there is no global governing body to make decisions about this planet's destiny. The global dark power emerges from the dark rooms, but it is not by any means a systematic application of laws for the good of the planet. It is simply an emerged form of power that applies against you automatically and autonomously. The only way to escape from this cursed bet is to wake up and demand a global governing body of wise people to make specific decisions, with the support of all of humanity and our organisations.

Thanks, dear reader. I have been very aggressive against you in this book and I am grateful to you because you displayed patience while reading this book. I am grateful to you because you helped me discover who I am: a creator of new worlds, a being who has advanced to the third phase of intelligence and the consciousness of the eternal continuum.

And what about you? Did you gain some profits by reading this book? A small share of power and knowledge? If yes, then I kindly ask you to post comment on Amazon to help other people through your profits.

Finally, we are at the end of this beautiful fantasy story of Noah, the amazing Animal Verse, which is based on real events.

See you in my third coming.

Appendix:

THE CONSTITUTIONAL ANOMALY OF SOUTH CYPRUS

Earlier, you found out a little about the horrible practices that occur in Cyprus. In this appendix, you'll find out what exactly this island of terror is about, with me as your personal tour guide. As someone who lives in south Cyprus, I will show you this parody state, an offshore country governed by an offshore president. South Cyprus is yet another example of straight-line velocity, where you saw earlier that humans support horrible practices merely because their government approves of it.

Southern Cyprus

First, you must understand that southern Cyprus is considered a 'state', but it is a special case indeed. I have extensively studied this very odd case and found that southern Cyprus does not have a sufficient legal framework and background to be considered a state. In reality, it is a perpetual international constitutional anomaly that merely calls itself a state. It does not meet any criteria to be a member of an international organisation. As such, it is an international constitutional anomaly.

Until 1959, Britain was the governor of Cyprus. In 1959, it was responsible for the constitutional transmission of Cyprus from colony status to state status. Unfortunately, the island's independence constitution of 1960 was very short-lived — with everyone involved taking care to dissect it in their own way — until it was rendered legally dead and void in 1963.

As the constitution collapsed in 1963, the state was cancelled and is therefore invalid. Since March 1964, there has been no constitutional framework governing the functioning of this supposed state. On the skeleton of the dead and invalid constitution, the southern Cypriots built the bizarre 'doctrine of necessity', which everything is referred to and operated under.

The state was 'saved' from collapse by Britain, when it persuaded the security council of the United Nations (UN) to recognise the Greek community as having international legal authority over the island, so it became known as the Republic of Cyprus. This recognition was backed by the resolution of the security council (number 186, March 1964). However, this resolution fell down in 1974.

It is my personal view that the recognition resolution fell down in July 1974 because a foreign country —Greece — violently cancelled it by invading in Cyprus, when the terrorist group EOKA-B committed the rape, torture, and genocide of Turkish Cypriots (which was designed long before 1974). Thankfully, NATO and the Turkish forces came together under the operational name Aishe, and because of this peaceful operation, the Turkish Cypriot community survived the genocide.[13]

The Nationalistic Sentiment

So, the Republic of Cyprus has de facto been cancelled since 1974, though it's possible that the UK together with the UN are working hard to rebuild a new state on the island. Of course, it's obvious that they face massive objections from

---

[13] In their latest provoking political action, the nationalistic regime of the South sent a member representative to the European parliament who is the daughter of the second in command of the terrorist group EOKA-B, the same terrorist group who killed, raped, and tortured thousands of Turkish Cypriot men, women, and children between 1971 and 1974. The UN blamed EOKA-B for their atrocities as criminals against humanity, but nobody was charged with any crime.

The grand designer of these events was Henry Kissinger, who is now almost 100 years old. His main worry, which pushed him to create these scary events and the tragedy of innocent people, was to remove any Russian influence from the island, to prevent it becoming the Cuba of the Mediterranean Sea.

This is discussed in various books from international analysts, who confirmed that the Secretary of the Department of States, Henry Kissinger, was the grand designer of all Cypriot operations in Summer 1974. Even as a child in 1974, I knew about the dark role of Kissinger. However, it's important to understand that I never judge him. I am convinced that under the circumstances in the period before 1974, his strategic plans were probably necessary applications.

the extremely nationalistic attitude of the south Cypriot administration who as well as being totally corrupt, are also the most nationalistic regime in the world.

Imagine a state that abandoned its own national anthem and instead uses the national anthem of Greece. Imagine a state that abandoned its own national flag and instead uses the national flag of Greece. Imagine a state that abandoned its national sovereignty by handing over leadership of the national guard – the army forces of the state – to Greek officers. What a parody state!

This nationalistic attitude is also easily spotted in the behaviour of the south Cyprus citizens. Don't even consider telling them they are not Greek in origin! Of course, not all citizens share this nationalistic attitude. I am one of these citizens, of course. But when I share my thesis with any of the fanatics from the South, I place myself in grave danger and become the victim of attacks. Recently, one fucking bastard fanatic from the South sent me a message after a discussion, saying that his "people will find me" anywhere I go and "punish me hard." This was purely because of my feelings against the mainstream nationalistic mentality of this fucking south part of the island.

It's essential for everybody to understand that this parody state does not exist. It is an unbelievable story of international carelessness, yet it is true. It is also a blatant case of the failure of international legal order. We understand what is required to be considered a state, a constitution that among other principles protects the freedom of expressing a thesis, or more simply freedom of expression.

There is no state entity of southern Cyprus and therefore it's obvious and essential that this parody state *must* cease to exist.

The Reason for Its Acceptance

All of this being the case, you might wonder why this international irregularity was accepted as a member of the EU and the Eurozone. Southern Cyprus neither geographically nor culturally belongs in Europe since it's clearly a mix of Middle Eastern, eastern Mediterranean, and English cultures in business. Yet it has established itself as a member state of the EU and the UN based on the mistaken acceptance of the constitutional anomaly by both organisations (while they still continue to ignore the existence of northern Cyprus, an issue we will look at shortly).

Another reason for the acceptance of southern Cyprus was the dark and deceptive practice of the American oligarchy to 'grab them so they don't end up in Russia's arms', as discussed earlier. Likewise, the German finance minister at the time — who was dealing with Russian deposits in southern Cyprus — believed he could eliminate the Russian element from the island. However, his efforts failed miserably. The Russian element is not only widespread on the island, but the vast majority of residents regard Russia not as a friendly country but not as its enemy country.[14]

---

[14] After the war in Ukraine began, the USA and the EU applied tons of pressure against the south Cyprus regime to abandon all of its relations with Russia, and the result is that Russia now considers the south Cypriot regime as its enemy.

And for these reasons, southern Cyprus, which geographically has barely any links to Europe and is not constitutionally sound, was found to be a member of the EU one morning and the Eurozone on another morning!

However, this case is of little concern to international analysts given the small size of the island. They have locked in their minds that southern Cyprus' exit from the Eurozone, whether unregulated or agreed, is manageable and will not cause any tension, neither a tsunami nor a domino effect. Of course, they don't care if Cyprus leaves the EU now because of the very small size of the south Cypriot economy, which is less than 0.2% of the total Eurozone economy.

Indeed, the EU institutions took actions to cancel any domino event by effectively isolating the island from the rest of the European space. They isolated the Cypriot banks from any other bank within the Eurosystem and forcibly alienated assets that were imposed in 2013 on Cypriot banks with branches in Greece.

This violent alienation occurred at the same time as the shameful practice of cutting deposits in southern Cypriot banks, known as the 'haircut'. During the 15 day banking pause for the haircut, the President of Cyprus moved €40 million out of the banking system for his family and his own deposits, suffering no haircut himself. This is why even the international media called him an 'offshore president'.

What puzzles me is why the citizens of this strange state accepted the dishonourable and criminal act of robbing their deposits while their president evaded it. Indeed, there are videos showing southern Cypriots having fun and unwinding at carnivals the very day after the haircut, almost headbutting each other in joy. Though, regardless of whether the citizens recognised their plight, atrocious acts were committed against innocent people by the corrupt regime of southern Cyprus, and we have still not seen anyone deal with these crimes, while the main culprit sits in guilty silence.

Later, the offshore president and his family created great money from the passport investment plan, which was pay and take. Pay the lawyers and other mediators, buy a house, and take on a European nationality. Through the president's law office in Limassol, hundreds of foreign people paid to receive European nationality. The family business of the offshore president gained sky-high profits by selling this European nationality to citizens.

Of course, the passport selling program stopped in 2020 after a shocking report was shown on the Al Jazeera channel where high-level officials were secretly filmed dealing with the sale of the European nationality to an unknown 'customer' from China! Among these officials was the president of the parliament. What a parody state indeed!

However, please note that the information throughout this book about the President of south Cyprus, including his dirty business and his bad fame, are all based on local and international media publications. Among these was the shocking documentary on the Al Jazeera channel, and of course the resolutions of the European parliament, European Commission announcements, and international research by various organisations, including the Pandora and Panama papers. Please note that I do not have any personal view on this and did not witness these events. I am totally outside such a dirty and corrupt regime and this book is by no means a book of research. I am not any judge authority, nor an investigating authority. I hope I am clear on that.

What I do believe is that south Cyprus is a travesty state, where everything dirty is permitted to happen. From money laundering to sex trafficking of women (as you learned about earlier), to selling the European nationality to thousands of fraudsters, gangsters, dictators, and money laundering all over the world through the corrupt 'passport investment plan'. What's more, a few months after the haircut, the 67-year-old (at the time) minister of economics was arrested by the police in a hotel in north Nicosia in bed with two boys aged 14 and 15 years old. What a travesty state indeed!

In this context of an alleged 'state', southern Cyprus represents itself and is like the owner of a huge economical exclusive zone, which is frightening in relation to the size of the island, and it neglects the existence of northern Cyprus. Let me emphasise this: Cyprus is *not* a state, has no constitution, has no Economical Exclusive Zone (EEZ), and is not a member of any international organisation. It cannot claim to be a state when there is no reference and no international legal provision for northern Cyprus perfectly and indefinitely.

Furthermore, conflicts in the eastern Mediterranean continue unabated between the USA and Russia. It is not clear who will prevail, but in either case southern Cyprus is not in a position to withstand competition within the Eurozone. I am certain that it will be financially and politically degraded, while the corrupt regime that governs it has no concern for the future of its indebted citizens.

Northern Cyprus

If you look beyond southern Cyprus, you will find northern Cyprus, although it's treated as if it doesn't exist. It's an area cut off from civilisation, from the rest of the world, as if its inhabitants are locked up as criminals in Alcatraz. Thankfully, I am determined to bring to light this case of seclusion from civilisation. To highlight the hypocrisy, the collective failure to treat it as the 'civilised thing' we claim it to be. Indeed, it is the only area in the Western world excluded and cut off from civilisation.

I visit northern Cyprus on regular basis because it is my lost self and I have found it to be one of the most magnetically attractive places on this planet. There, I am free from the fetters of the tyranny of the Eurozone. The north is not a member of this dictatorship of a common currency with those whom they have nothing in common, so I go there to breathe fresh air and enjoy my freedom.

It is a beautiful area endowed by our Earth with a magnetic arc. At one moment, it captivates you with the eerie atmosphere it creates and the next it takes you to the ends of spiritual pleasure and contemplation. The complete north-east coast of the island is in a magnetic vortex unique to the entire planet. I also experienced the same euphoria in the southern part of the island, in the coastal area south to the south-east, which is the vortex area between Limassol and Larnaca, the coastal areas south of the motorway, well-known for its seaside, natural beauty, and fish taverns almost leaning against the waves.

Magnetic vortexes, for the mystics of the spiritual powers, are areas of nature's miracles, which create an environment suitable for practicing contemplation in the higher spheres, and discovering new knowledge, new powers, and new natural laws not described in the physics books of scientists.

Indeed, this entire region of the world — the eastern Mediterranean — historically and culturally created cultures such as Egyptian, Phoenician, Jewish, Arab, Ottoman, and others. In this region, Jesus of Nazareth was born and taught, according to the scriptures (though I often dispute the content of the scriptures), Jesus in whose name one of the great religions of the world was created.

Therefore, I propose several solutions to resolve the issue of northern and southern Cyprus. It is my responsibility to make this matter a global priority and to bring an end to this international constitutional anomaly. I believe that we can make a decisive contribution to the annulment of the current international legal status of Cyprus in the minds of the people, as well as those responsible.

Solution One

My solution to the Cyprus problem is this: south Cyprus must return to its previous status, but not as colony — as part of the UK with financial and political autonomy. This would be the best solution for NATO and the USA!

South Cyprus must become a neutral zone for trading, science, technology, and land development. In this way, it can become a peaceful multi-civilisation with companies from all over the world choosing to have their base there. In some ways, this is already happening, but this new state must abandon the nationalistic local population of the 'aboriginal' fanatics.

Limassol must also be protected as a top priority, as the world multi-civilisation prototype city. Limassol is the only city in the world where in one restaurant or bar, you can meet people from Russia, Ukraine, UK, USA, Europe, Israel, Gulf countries, China, and Latin America. You will find these people around the world in various places, but only in Limassol will you find them sitting peacefully and enjoying their time without any problems.

Here, they realise that the citizens of the world have nothing to fight about between each other and only share the place where they live, planet Earth. People without politicians can sit perfectly and peacefully together, not seeing each other as enemies, and my evidence is the city of Limassol, the city where I live.

Here, I abandon my neutralisation and take my direction to the new and popular king of the UK, King Charles III. South Cyprus would be the diamond of the crown, though a fake little diamond! In this case, a diamond means probable huge natural gas sources from the surrounding seas of the island, especially the south seas of the island, but this is only probable, OK? The oil companies in charge must decide on the commercial values of the deposits already found and the discoveries of new deposits will follow.

The UK, NATO, and USA must secure political control of the island, not in a disastrous way, like their previous decision to accept the island as a member of the EU, but in a harmonious way by accepting the south part of the island as part of the UK.

In this case, north Cyprus and Turkey will decide their own political fate and destiny.

Solution Two

In the second possible solution, BlackRock could buy south Cyprus. Does this sound shocking to you? Well, it doesn't to me. During the bailout rescue of the south Cypriot economy in 2013, the rescue team were Troika (Troika actually means three): the IMF, the ECB, and the European Commission. This fundamental team provided the necessary funds and assignment of national sovereignty from the rescued south Cyprus state to its international lenders. The terms of assignment of sovereignty were included as an essential term in the so-called 'memorandum of understanding', which is now a law of the state after the approval of its terms by parliament.

So, BlackRock may come to an agreement with the assembly of the lenders (which are now the ESM, the ECB, and the international investors who invested in the south Cypriot state bonds under the English Law) to buy south Cyprus. The total public debt of the state is €24 billion. I estimate that an investor could buy the state for around €44 billion, similar to what Twitter cost Elon Musk.

With this deal, which would be the first in history, a member nation of the UN would move under the ownership of a big world investment group, and the brand name of the country would pass under the ownership of the investor. This would be no worries for its citizens. The investor would buy the brand name, not any private lands and premises, not anyone's private interests, nor any private company or bank. For me, the ideal investor would be the superstars BlackRock and this deal may prove to be the most successful investment ever.

This way, the south part of the island would become a neutral political entity and steadily emerge as the number one firm and centre in the world for multinational, multi-civilisational science, technology, trading, and tourism. The south part of the island, which is located at the corner of three continents — Asia, Africa, and Europe — will emerge as a place of peace, progress, and cooperation between the East and the West, between all the giants of the world. It will leave the rest to fight each other elsewhere if they wish, while it will live in the permanent Olympic games of peace.

It will have a vision, and personally I would love to observe the process and evolution of such a gigantic vision, to improve the life of the struggling humanity — to work together on all global challenges to find solutions for the public's interests. It is an experiment on how the planet could be a better place to live and how the future of the residents of this planet may one day arise, free from the bonds of the tyranny of our human animal nature.

What a blessing solution for me! God bless BlackRock.

REFERENCES

i https://probion.com/probion-blog/how-much-toxic-waste-is-trapped-in-your-body

ii https://edition.cnn.com/2016/05/17/health/sti-infanticide-human-monogamy/index.html

iii https://storyteller.travel/animals-that-mate-for-life/

iv https://www.unodc.org/documents/data-and-analysis/statistics/crime/UN_BriefFem_251121.pdf.

v https://rapecrisis.org.uk/get-informed/statistics-sexual-violence/.

vi An article from *Scientific American* stated:

"The White House announced this morning that the U.S. will rapidly increase exports of liquefied natural gas to Europe as Germany and other E.U. nations try to diminish their dependence on Russian fossil fuels.

The move will ramp up LNG shipments carried by seagoing tankers by 15 billion cubic meters this year, according to a fact sheet released by the White House. As a comparison, the United States sent 22 bcm of LNG to Europe last year, the highest ever traded between the two continents.

The announcement promises to raise concerns about the trajectory of global climate action. The construction of LNG terminals and other infrastructure could put the U.S. and other nations on a path toward using gas for years to come, even as those countries strive to phase out fossil fuels, advocates warn.

The White House said American exports of LNG will continue to grow through 2030, by which time the U.S. plans to be sending 50 billion cubic meters of gas to Europe annually.

"This build-out will occur in a way that is consistent with, not in conflict with, the net-zero climate goal that we're shooting for," Biden said during a meeting with European officials in Brussels this morning. He called the effort a 'catalyst' for doubling down on investments in clean energy.

Biden also spoke with European leaders yesterday about ways to accelerate the transition toward clean energy, according to the White House.

In addition to working with other countries to bring new sources of LNG to Europe, the effort announced this morning—which will be overseen by a joint U.S.-E.U. task force—will involve helping the continent reduce demand for natural gas over the next two winters through energy efficiency measures and the build-out of clean energy.

A senior administration official speaking on background to reporters said today's announcement would help accelerate Europe's move away from Russian gas. He also said it would advance efforts to phase out gas in the U.S., which has a goal of halving greenhouse gas emissions by 2030."

vii https://www.bloomberg.com/opinion/articles/2022-12-15/qatar-the-world-cup-and-bribery-why-does-the-european-parliament-even-exist